INDIAN COOKERY

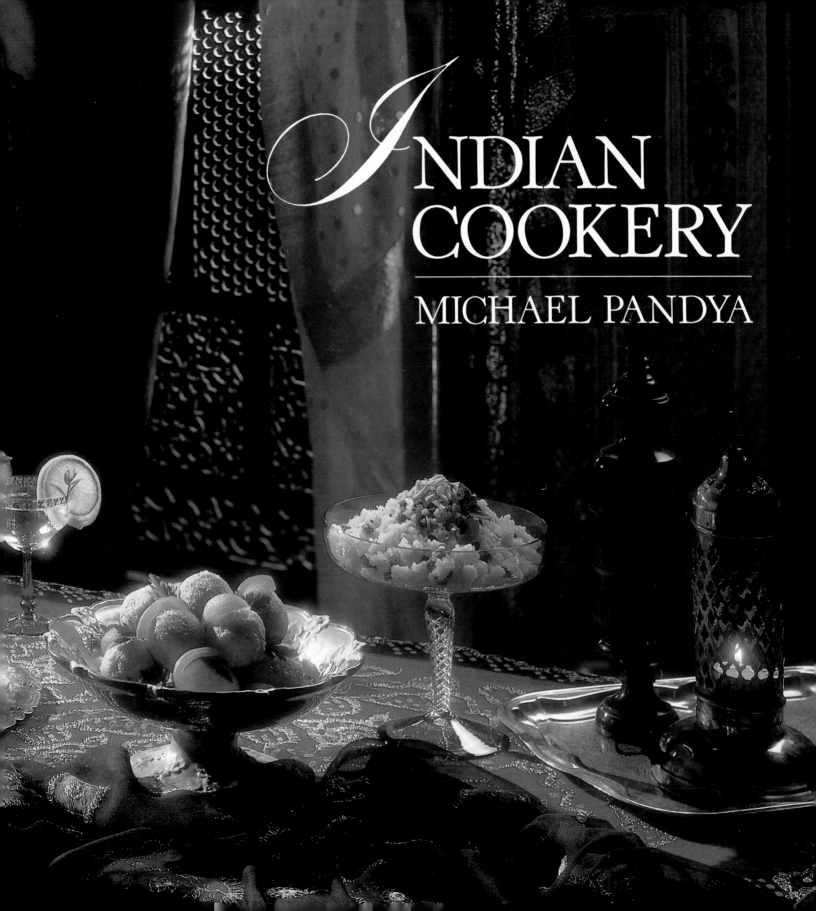

Indian Cookery

MICHAEL PANDYA

NOTE

1. All recipes serve four unless otherwise stated.

2. All spoon measurements are level. Spoon measures can be bought in both imperial and metric sizes to give accurate measurement of small quantities.

3. All eggs are size 2 or 3 unless otherwise stated.

4. All sugar is granulated unless otherwise stated.

5. Preparation times are an average calculated during recipe testing.

6. Metric and imperial measurements have been calculated separately. Use one set of measurements only as they are not exact equivalents.

7. Cooking times may vary slightly depending on the individual oven. Dishes should be placed in the centre of an oven unless otherwise specified.

8. Always preheat the oven or grill to the specified temperature.

9. If using a fan-assisted oven, follow the manufacturer's instructions for guidance on temperature adjustments.

First published in this edition by
The Octopus Publishing Group
Michelin House, 81 Fulham Road, London SW3 6RB
© 1988 Hennerwood Publications Ltd

ISBN 0 86273 4940

Printed in Italy

CONTENTS

SOUPS AND SNACKS

In an Indian meal there is no real equivalent to the Western starter, though even in India soups are now increasingly served as a separate first course. Snacks are eaten at any time of the day and there are even special stalls and shops to sell these delicacies, which are usually served with an array of chutneys and spices.

LEFT: Yam foogath for the brave; RIGHT: Samosas

SHAKAHARI GHORAMGHOR
VEGETARIAN MINESTRONE SOUP

25 g (1 oz) ghee
1 large onion, chopped
2 garlic cloves, crushed
1 large carrot, diced
1 large turnip, diced
1 celery stick, chopped
2 tablespoons peas, fresh or frozen
100 g (4 oz) white cabbage, shredded
4 large tomatoes, peeled and sliced
2 teaspoons salt
900 ml (1½ pints) vegetable stock
40 g (1½ oz) spaghetti
½ teaspoon freshly ground black pepper
1 tablespoon chopped coriander leaves

Preparation time: 10 minutes
Cooking time: 25 minutes

Since southern India has always been pre-dominantly vegetarian, the first soups made were introduced to suit those needs. Soups are often used in India as a substitute for a main course, perhaps as a light meal for invalids.

1. Heat the ghee in a saucepan and fry the onion and garlic until golden. Add the carrot, turnip, celery and peas and cook for 3 minutes. Stir in the cabbage, tomatoes, salt and stock and bring to the boil.
2. Reduce the heat, add the spaghetti, broken into small pieces, and pepper and simmer for 15 minutes. Sprinkle with chopped coriander before serving.

GOLGAPPA or PUCHKA
HOLLOW CRISPY WAFERS

SERVES 6
225 g (8 oz) flour
100 g (4 oz) semolina
50 g (2 oz) urad dall flour
2 teaspoons ghee, melted
water to bind
oil for deep frying
2 tablespoons cooked or canned chick peas

To serve (optional):
salt
a little red chilli powder

Preparation time: 45 minutes
Cooking time: 30 minutes

This is an ideal low-calorie savoury dish for weight-watchers, and of course others, too! Served with chick peas these delicate wafers have quite a unique flavour! Each one is eaten whole. One could eat dozens without feeling guilty.

1. Mix the flour, semolina and dall flour with the ghee and knead, gradually adding the minimum of water to make a stiff dough. Cover with a damp cloth and leave for about 30 minutes.
2. Knead the dough for 2–3 minutes and divide it into 4 portions. Roll each portion into a ball and then, applying a little of the oil and greasing the surface, roll each one into as large and thin a round as possible.
3. Using a pastry cutter, cut the dough into 3 cm (1½ inch) rounds. Roll these out again to smooth their edges and keep them covered with a damp cloth.
4. Heat the oil in a deep pan to 180°C, 350°F, or until a cube of bread browns in 30 seconds. Slide in 4 rounds at a time and cook until they are golden brown on both sides and puffed up. To help the discs puff up, make slight waves in the oil by holding a ladle perpendicularly in the middle of the pan and gently shaking it. Reduce the heat from time to time so that the oil does not become too hot.
5. Drain the cooked golgappas on absorbent kitchen paper and leave them to cool. Make a hole in the top of each one and fill with chick peas. If required, sprinkle salt or chilli powder on top of each helping.

LEFT: Vegetarian minestrone soup; RIGHT: Hollow crispy wafers

AALU KI TIKIYA
POTATO CHAAT

450 g (1 lb) potatoes, boiled, peeled and
 mashed
salt
½ teaspoon garam masala
1 teaspoon coarsely chopped coriander
1 small onion, peeled and finely chopped
2 green chillies, chopped
½ teaspoon grated fresh ginger root
ghee for frying
Chaat spices (see right)

Preparation time: 30 minutes
Cooking time: about 15 minutes

The addiction of people in India to chaat shops can be likened to the adult addiction to pubs in the West. A chaat shop usually opens early in the evening and is well stocked with the main goodies and the chaat spices, i.e. salt, pounded red chillies, garam masala, black salt and roasted and ground cumin seeds, which the customer mixes to taste and sprinkles over the food. There is also supply of tamarind juice and yogurt mixture (yogurt beaten in half of its weight of water).

1. Mix together the potatoes, salt, garam masala, coriander, onion, chillies and ginger.
2. Divide the mixture into 8 portions and shape each portion into a thick round.
3. Heat a little ghee in a heavy frying pan.

Fry the potato chops in 2 batches. Cook for about 4 minutes on each side, until golden brown.
4. Mix together the chaat spices, sprinkle over the chops and serve with a selection of chutneys.

CHILLIES
Red chillies, an essential ingredient in the spice mixture customarily served with chaat dishes – themselves an integral element of Indian life – are not native to India at all. Belonging to the capsicum family, chillies originate in Mexico, and were brought to India in the sixteenth century by Portuguese traders. Over the years their peppery, fiery flavour has been exploited with much sophistication, and now India is the world's chief exporter of chillies.

SONTH PAKODI
PAKODI IN TAMARIND SAUCE

SERVES 6
450 g (1 lb) gram flour
450 ml (¾ pint) water
½ teaspoon salt
1 green chilli, chopped
pinch of baking powder
vegetable oil for frying
tamarind sauce
300 ml (½ pint) plain yogurt
Chaat spices (see above)

Preparation time: 30 minutes
Cooking time: 20 minutes

1. Beat together the flour and 300 ml (½ pint) water to make a thick batter. Stir in ½ teaspoon salt, the chilli and baking powder.
2. Heat the oil in a frying pan over medium heat. Add 1 teaspoon of batter at a time to make the pakodas; cook several at a time. Fry on both sides until golden brown. Remove and drain on kitchen paper until cool.
3. Soak the pakodas in warm water for 10 minutes, then squeeze them out.
4. Mix together the chaat spices with the tamarind sauce and the yogurt beaten with 150 ml (¼ pint) water. Toss the pakodas in this mixture and serve.

TOP: Potato chaat;
BOTTOM: Pakodi in tamarind sauce

ANDAA KACHOOMAR
INDIAN SCRAMBLED EGGS

6 eggs
1 medium onion, chopped
1 teaspoon grated root ginger
2 green chillies, chopped
salt
½ teaspoon freshly ground black pepper
100 g (4 oz) ghee
2 tomatoes, peeled and sliced
1 tablespoon chopped coriander leaves
thinly sliced cucumber, to garnish

Preparation time: 10 minutes
Cooking time: 10 minutes

This dish is so quick to make it's ideal for a busy cook. If you are starving and have no time to prepare elaborate dishes, eat this with bread and Indian pickles.

1. Beat the eggs together in a bowl for 2 minutes. Mix in the onion, ginger, chillies, salt and pepper.
2. Heat the ghee in a frying pan over a moderate heat. Pour in the egg mixture and cook, stirring continuously, for about 3–5 minutes or until the egg thickens and sets. Add the tomatoes and mix well. Serve with coriander and cucumber.

DHOKHA
DELUSION FRITTERS

2 green chillies, finely chopped
1 teaspoon baking powder
2 medium onions, chopped
15 g (½ oz) root ginger, grated
salt
8 garlic cloves, crushed
450 g (1 lb) gram flour
1 teaspoon garam masala
1 teaspoon carom seeds
1 teaspoon white cumin seeds
250 ml (8 fl oz) water
100 g (4 oz) ghee
½ teaspoon turmeric powder
1 teaspoon red chilli powder
1 teaspoon ground coriander

To garnish:
2 teaspoons lemon juice
2 tablespoons chopped coriander leaves

Preparation time: 20 minutes
Cooking time: 35 minutes

This is a remarkable dish in that the fritters can be used as a snack or side dish and can be curried too. They are most enjoyable as a teatime savoury – I used to love them as a child and still do to this day.

1. Mix together the chillies, baking powder, half the onion, the ginger, salt, garlic, gram flour, the garam masala, carom and cumin seeds and the water. Knead the mixture throughly and shape into 8 equal sausage shapes, about 2.5 cm (1 inch) in diameter.
2. Bring a saucepan of water to the boil and cook the sausage shapes for 10–15 minutes. When cooked, remove the shapes with a slotted spoon. Drain the sausages well and leave them to cool. Cut them into 1 cm (½ inch) slices.
3. Heat the ghee in a frying pan and fry the remaining onion until it is golden brown. Add the turmeric, chilli powder and coriander and stir well. Add the sausage slices and stir over a low heat for 10 minutes, taking care not to break the pieces.
4. Pour the lemon juice over the fritters and sprinkle them with the chopped coriander before serving.

LEFT: Indian scrambled eggs; RIGHT: Delusion fritters

ADRAK SOUP
GINGER SOUP

25 g (1 oz) root ginger, peeled and grated
900 ml (1½ pints) water
1 teaspoon salt
1 tablespoon white cumin seeds, roasted and
  ground
½ teaspoon freshly ground black pepper
3 tablespoons lemon juice

Preparation time: 5 minutes
Cooking time: 35 minutes

This is a rather unusual soup and you have to acquire a taste for it. It gives you inner warmth and is particularly good served on a cold winter's day.

1. Place the ginger in a saucepan, add the water and bring it to the boil. Leave it to simmer over a low heat for about 30 minutes until the water is reduced to half.
2. Add the salt and ground cumin and cook for a further 2 minutes. Remove the pan from the heat, sprinkle with the pepper and transfer to individual bowls. Pour a little lemon juice on each serving. Serve hot.

KEEMA SAMOSA
MINCED MEAT SAMOSA

SERVES 6
450 g (1 lb) plain flour
1 teaspoon salt
175 g (6 oz) soft margarine
150 ml (¼ pint) water
2 tablespoons milk
oil for deep frying
chutney, to serve

Filling:
1 tablespoon butter
1 small onion, chopped
½ teaspoon white cumin seeds
225 g (8 oz) minced beef
1 green chilli, finely chopped
1 teaspoon salt
100 g (4 oz) cooked peas
pinch of freshly ground black pepper
1 teaspoon chopped coriander leaves

Preparation time: 1 hour
Cooking time: 30 minutes

TOP: Ginger soup; BOTTOM: Minced meat samosas

This dish is a snack which can be eaten hot or cold. It is good served at parties, with drinks, for tea or picnics. The dish is popular throughout the continent of Asia and, I suspect, beyond!

1. To make the pastry, sift the flour and salt into a large bowl. Add the margarine to the flour, rubbing it in until the mixture resembles fine breadcrumbs. Stir in the water, a little at a time, and knead until a hard dough is formed. Cover the dough with a damp cloth and leave for about 15 minutes.
2. To make the filling, melt the butter in a saucepan and add the onion and cumin seeds. Stir over a moderate heat for 5–7 minutes. Add the mince, chilli and salt and mix thoroughly. Reduce the heat and cook for a further 10 minutes, stirring occasionally.
3. Add the peas and stir them in. Leave over a moderate heat for 5 minutes or until all the liquid has evaporated. Remove the pan from the heat, add the pepper and chopped coriander and mix thoroughly. Leave the filling to cool before use.

4. Divide the dough into 12 equal portions. Roll each one out to a thin 18 cm (7 inch) diameter round. Cut each round through the middle using a sharp kitchen knife. Cover these semi-circles with a clean damp cloth while you are filling them, one at a time.
5. Take 1 semi-circle and brush the edges with milk. With the semi-circle on a flat surface, spoon some cooled filling into the centre and fold in the corners, overlapping them to form a cone. Fold over and seal the top to make a triangle. Repeat the process with all of the semi-circles to use up all the filling. Cover the prepared samosas with a damp cloth, keeping them separated from each other.
6. Heat the oil in a deep pan to 180°C, 350°F, or until a cube of bread browns in 30 seconds. Slide 4 samosas at a time into the oil. Reduce the heat a little and fry the samosas until they are light brown on both sides. Take care when turning them over that the filling does not escape.
7. Remove the cooked samosas from the pan and drain them on absorbent kitchen paper. Serve hot with chutney.

ALOO SAMOSA
VEGETABLE SAMOSA

SERVES 6
1 tablespoon ghee
pinch of asafoetida powder
2 teaspoons mustard seeds
450 g (1 lb) potatoes, parboiled and diced
100 g (4 oz) cooked peas
2 green chillies, chopped
1½ teaspoons salt
1 teaspoon pomegranate seeds
1 teaspoon garam masala
2 tablespoons chopped coriander leaves

Preparation time: 1 hour
Cooking time: 30 minutes

These pasties are cooked in exactly the same way as Keema samosas, but with a vegetarian filling. Use the same pastry as for Keema samosas (page 15) and form and fill the pasties in the same way.

1. Heat the ghee in a frying pan and add the asafoetida powder, mustard seeds, potatoes, peas, chillies, salt and pomegranate seeds. Stir well over a moderate heat for about 2 minutes. Cover the pan, reduce the heat and leave to cook for about 10 minutes.
2. Add the garam masala and coriander and stir well. Allow the filling to cool before use.
3. Prepare and cook the pastries as for Keema samosas, steps 4-7 (page 15). Serve hot with your favourite sauce or chutney.

RAJVIR ARBI GAPODE
YAM FOOGATH FOR THE BRAVE

225 g (8 oz) cooked yams
225 g (8 oz) potatoes, parboiled
1 teaspoon salt
1 teaspoon mustard oil
1 teaspoon mustard seeds
1 tablespoon chopped coriander leaves
1 tablespoon grated coconut
1 small onion, peeled and chopped
1 green chilli, chopped
1 teaspoon grated root ginger
vegetable oil for deep frying

Batter:
3 tablespoons chick pea flour
4 tablespoons water

To serve:
Chutney or sauce

Preparation time: 20 minutes
Cooking time: 40 minutes

Foogath is the name given to a dish which uses the leftovers of an already cooked vegetable or meat dish. In this way you can curry up the leftovers of the Sunday roast or the remains of a vegetable bhaji. There are three essential ingredients for a foogath: some cooked leftovers, coconut and mustard oil for frying. Cook yams the same way as you would potatoes.

1. Using a fork, mash the yams and potatoes together and add the salt.
2. Heat the oil in a frying pan and add the mustard seeds. Add the potato and yam mixture to the pan with the coriander, coconut, onion, chilli and ginger. Stir over a low heat for about 10 minutes. Remove the pan from the heat and allow the mixture to cool. Form the mixture into 12 small balls.
3. Heat the oil to 180°C, 350°F, or until a cube of bread browns in 30 seconds. Make a batter by mixing the chick pea flour with the water until smooth. Coat the balls in the batter and fry them in the oil until they are light brown. Serve with a chutney or sauce of your choice.

TOP: Vegetable samosas; BOTTOM: Yam foogath for the brave

HARI DHANIA KE AALU
POTATO IN GREEN CORIANDER

*450 g (1 lb) small potatoes, boiled and
  skinned*
4 tablespoons fresh coriander leaves
1 teaspoon salt
4 green chillies
6 tablespoons lemon juice

Preparation time: 15 minutes, plus
cooking potatoes

1. Prick the potatoes all over evenly and
lightly with a cocktail stick so that they will
absorb the flavour of the coriander paste.
Be careful not to break them.
2. Grind the coriander leaves with the salt,
green chillies and lemon juice to make a
thin paste. This is most easily done in a
pestle and mortar; otherwise use a wooden
spoon in an earthenware bowl.

3. When the paste has reached an even
consistency smear it thickly over the
potatoes and leave them to stand for 2
minutes.
4. Serve as a snack or appetiser, with cocktail sticks.

MATAR CHAAT
DRIED PEAS CHAAT

SERVES 6
225 g (8 oz) dried peas, soaked overnight
water as necessary
½ teaspoon baking powder
pinch of asafoetida powder
Chaat spices (see page 11)

To serve:
tamarind sauce
whipped dahi (see page 134)

Preparation time: 10 minutes, plus
soaking
Cooking time: 15–20 minutes

1. Drain the peas and place them in a
saucepan with enough water to cover, together with baking powder and asafoetida.
Cook over a medium heat for 15–20
minutes, until tender. Drain.
2. Sprinkle with chaat spices to taste, and
serve with tamarind sauce and whipped
dahi. Crumble a few golgappas (see page
8) over the dish if desired.

TAMARIND
*Tamarinds or imli belong to the pea family, and
have been grown in all parts of India for
hundreds of years. They are sold with the pods
intact, but it is the brown pulp inside,
surrounding the seeds, which is the useful part. It
can be eaten fresh; alternatively the pods can be
soaked and then squeezed to extract the juice from
the pulp to make tamarind water. The sharp and
refreshing flavour of this liquid is as widely used
in Indian dishes as lemon juice is in European
recipes. It can be combined with yogurt as a
cooling drink, and features also in sauces and
chutneys.*

*LEFT: Potato in green coriander; RIGHT: Dried peas
chaat*

RICE AND PULSES

Pulses (lentils, beans and peas) and rice are used widely in Indian cooking. Pulses are used to make the delicately flavoured dhals, served with rice or bread, or are even cooked with other vegetables, meat or fish to make a hearty stew. Rice, cultivated in India for some 6000 years, is one of the staple foods of the country.

LEFT: *Vegetable biriyani;* RIGHT: *Chick pea chops*

TOOR DALL
PIGEON PEA PURÉE

175 g (6 oz) ghee
6 garlic cloves, crushed
2 medium onions, peeled, chopped and
    crushed
1 teaspoon turmeric powder
225 g (8 oz) pigeon peas
900 ml (1½ pints) water
salt
1 teaspoon white cumin seeds
1 green mango, peeled and sliced
1 green chilli, chopped
pinch of asafoetida powder
½ teaspoon red chilli powder

To garnish:
2 tablespoons chopped coriander leaves

Preparation time: 15 minutes
Cooking time: 1 hour

A vegetarian kachcha meal is incomplete without a dhal. This is one of the most popular – eat it with chapatis or rice.

1. Heat 50 g (2 oz) ghee in a saucepan and fry the garlic and half the onions until golden brown. Stir in the turmeric, pigeon peas and water. Add salt to taste. Simmer, covered, for about 30 minutes.
2. Add the mango slices to the pigeon pea mixture and cook for a further 15–20 minutes. Transfer the mixture to a casserole and keep it hot.
3. Heat the remaining ghee and fry the rest of the onion with the cumin seeds until they are golden brown. Remove the pan from the heat and add the green chilli, asafoetida and red chilli powder. Mix well and pour over the dhal mixture in the cas-serole. Serve hot, garnished with the chopped coriander.

SAADA CHAAWAL PULLAO
PLAIN RICE PULLAO

225 g (8 oz) long-grain rice
100 g (4 oz) ghee
1 large onion, peeled and thinly sliced
2 bay leaves
4 cloves
6 black peppercorns
1 × 2.5 cm (1 inch) piece cinnamon stick
1 brown cardamom
½ teaspoon turmeric powder
2 tomatoes, peeled and sliced
1 teaspoon salt
600 ml (1 pint) water
50 g (2 oz) butter
pinch of saffron strands steeped in 1
    teaspoon hot water

Preparation time: 25 minutes
Cooking time: 25 minutes

This dish is also known as Kesaria pullao or saffron rice. It is a more sophisticated rice preparation, usually served with non-vegetarian meals, or on special occasions with vegetarian ones.

1. Wash the rice and soak it in water for 20 minutes. Heat the ghee and fry half the onion with the bay leaves, cloves, pepper-corns, cinnamon and cardamom until golden brown.
2. Drain the rice and add it to the ghee mixture with the turmeric and tomatoes. Stir thoroughly and add the salt gradually. Add the water, bring to the boil and leave over a low heat for 10 minutes, or until the water is absorbed and the rice is tender.
3. Sprinkle the saffron water over the rice mixture. Fry the remaining onion slices in the butter until they are crisp and brown and scatter them over the rice pullao to serve.

LEFT: Pigeon pea purée; RIGHT: Plain rice pullao

MASAALA DOSA
STUFFED DHOSA

SERVES 6

100 g (4 oz) split black beans, soaked overnight
225 g (8 oz) rice, soaked overnight
pinch of baking powder
½ teaspoon salt
vegetable oil, for frying

Stuffing:
1 tablespoon ghee
1 teaspoon mustard seed
½ teaspoon turmeric
1 large onion, peeled and chopped
225 g (8 oz) potatoes, boiled, peeled and diced
6 curry leaves
½ teaspoon salt
½ teaspoon chilli powder

Preparation time: 30 minutes, plus soaking overnight
Cooking time: about 20 minutes and standing time

An attractive South India dish which can be eaten with or without stuffing. It is usually served hot with coconut chutney and Saambhar sauce (see page 32).

1. To make the stuffing, heat the ghee in a pan and add the mustard seed. Stir for 1 minute then add the turmeric, onion, potatoes, and curry leaves. Sprinkle on the salt and chilli powder, cover the pan and simmer for about 5 minutes until well blended, stirring from time to time. Keep the stuffing warm until required.

2. Drain the black beans and rice and grind in a food processor to a frothy pouring consistency. Add the baking powder and salt and mix thoroughly. Leave to stand for 30 minutes.
3. Warm a griddle over moderate heat, drop ½ teaspoon of oil in it, then pour on 1 tablespoon of the batter. Quickly spread out the batter with a spatula. Cook for a few minutes, then turn and cook on the other side, making sure it does not burn.
4. Leaving the dhosa on the griddle, spread 2 tablespoons of stuffing down the middle. Fold over the sides and serve hot with Saambhar sauce (see page 32). Make the remaining stuffed dhosas in the same way.

KABAB ALLAHABADI
CHICK CHOPS

SERVES 6

450 g (1 lb) chick peas
900 ml (1½ pints) water
1 large onion, peeled and chopped
50 g (2 oz) root ginger, coarsely chopped
10 garlic cloves, crushed
2½ teaspoons salt
100 g (4 oz) ghee
Spice mixture (see page 132)
1 medium onion, peeled and finely chopped
2 green chillies, finely chopped
3.5 cm (1½ inch) root ginger, grated
2 tablespoons chopped coriander leaves
1 egg, beaten
2 lemons, sliced

TOP: Stuffed dhosa; BOTTOM: Chick chops

Preparation time: 30 minutes, plus soaking overnight
Cooking time: 30 minutes

1. Soak the chick peas overnight in water. Remove and discard any which have not softened. Drain the chick peas and mix them with the measured water, onion, ginger, garlic and salt together with the spice mixture and bring to the boil. When the chick peas are tender enough to crush between the thumb and finger, remove them from the heat and leave them to cool.
2. Drain off any excess water and grind the remaining mixture to a purée or process it in a blender. Combine the purée with the onion, green chilli, ginger, coriander and beaten egg. Divide the mixture into 18 portions and form them into round cakes.

3. Heat the ghee in a frying pan and fry the chick chops on both sides until golden brown. Garnish with slices of lemon and serve with a sauce of your choice.

MASOOR KI DALL
LENTILS

SERVES 6
225 g (8 oz) lentils
1.2 litres (2 pints) water
salt
175 g (6 oz) ghee
1 large onion, peeled and chopped
1 green chilli, chopped
½ teaspoon red chilli powder
1 teaspoon white cumin seeds
pinch of asafoetida powder

Preparation time: 15 minutes
Cooking time: 2 hours

There is a saying in Hindi which means that you have to have a special mouth before you are entitled to share the experience of eating this dhal.

1. Wash the lentils in cold, running water. Drain them and add to the measured water in a saucepan, with salt to taste. Simmer for 1½ hours.
2. Heat 65 g (2½ oz) of the ghee in a separate saucepan and fry the onion until it is golden brown. Add the green chilli and red chilli powder. When the lentils are tender and cooked, add the onion mixture to the pan and simmer for a further 10 minutes. Transfer the dhal to 6 individual bowls.
3. Heat the remaining ghee with the cumin seeds and asafoetida powder for about 30 seconds and pour about 1 tablespoon over each bowl to serve.
4. Serve immediately as a first course, with bread, or as a spicy accompaniment to curry.

SABZIYON KI BIRIYANI
VEGETABLE BIRIYANI

3 tablespoons ghee or vegetable oil
1 large onion, finely chopped
2 cloves garlic, peeled and chopped
8 cloves
2 × 2.5 cm (1 inch) cinnamon sticks
4 green cardamom pods
1 teaspoon turmeric
1 teaspoon garam masala
450 g (1 lb) Basmati rice, pre-soaked
225 g (8 oz) diced mixed vegetables
salt
600 ml (1 pint) vegetable stock
50 g (2 oz) paneer, lightly fried
100 g (4 oz) mixed nuts (cashews, almonds,
  pistachios, chopped)
50 g (2 oz) sultanas

Preparation time: 30 minutes
Cooking time: about 35 minutes

1. Heat the ghee or oil in a large pan and fry the onion until golden. Remove half for garnish. Add the garlic and spices and fry for 2-3 minutes.
2. Rinse the rice in several changes of water and drain, then add to the pan, stir well and cook for another 5 minutes until translucent.
3. Add the vegetables and salt, add the stock and bring to a gradual boil. Cover, reduce the heat to very low and cook until all the liquid has been absorbed and the rice is cooked.
4. Add the cheese, mixed nuts and sultanas, mix well and cover. Cook for 5 more minutes over low heat until the moisture is all gone. Serve hot, sprinkled with the reserved onion.

LEFT: Lentils;
RIGHT: Vegetable biriyani

MATAR PANEER PULLAO
PEA AND CREAM CHEESE PULLAO

450 g (1 lb) long-grain rice
200 g (7 oz) ghee
1 large onion, peeled and finely chopped
4 bay leaves
6 cloves
8 black peppercorns
1 × 5 cm (2 inch) piece cinnamon stick
4 green cardamoms, crushed
1 black cardamom
1 teaspoon black cumin seeds
½ teaspoon turmeric powder
1 × 100 g (4 oz) packet frozen peas
1 medium potato, peeled and sliced
225 g (8 oz) paneer (see page 138), cubed
  and fried
1 green chilli, chopped
1½ teaspoon salt
1 teaspoon garam masala
4 tomatoes, peeled and sliced
2 hard-boiled eggs, sliced
1 tablespoon chopped coriander leaves

Preparation time: 1 hour
Cooking time: 35 minutes

This pullao has more flavour and distinction than a plain pullao. It is served as a special treat and goes rather well with a vegetarian meal.

1. Wash the rice and soak it in water for 30 minutes. Heat 175 g (6 oz) ghee in a frying pan and add half the chopped onion, the bay leaves, cloves, peppercorns, cinnamon, cardamoms and cumin seeds. Fry until golden. Add the turmeric, peas, potato, paneer and green chilli and fry for 10 minutes.
2. Drain the rice. Place it in a separate saucepan with the salt and boil it in plenty of water until half cooked. Drain the rice and stir it into the spice mixture. Add the garam masala and stir gently.

3. Arrange the tomato and egg slices on top of the rice and sprinkle with 2 teaspoons hot water and the chopped coriander. Cover with a tightly fitting lid and leave over a low heat for 5–7 minutes or until the rice is fully cooked.
4. Heat the remaining ghee and fry the remaining onion until golden. Serve the finished dish with the onion scattered on top.

CHANA URAD DALL
GRAM AND BLACK BEAN DHAL

SERVES 6
100 g (4 oz) split grams
100 g (4 oz) skinless dried black beans
salt
½ teaspoon turmeric powder
100 g (4 oz) marrow flesh
100 g (4 oz) ghee
1 medium onion, peeled and finely chopped
6 garlic cloves, crushed
1 teaspoon white cumin seeds
1 green chilli, chopped
1 dry red chilli, crushed
½ teaspoon red chilli powder

Preparation time: 15 minutes
Cooking time: 2 hours

This recipe gives a thick dhal.

1. Boil 1.2 litres (2 pints) of water in a saucepan. Wash the grams and beans under cold, running water and drain well. Add them to the boiling water with the salt and turmeric. Bring the water back to the boil. Cover the pan and simmer for 1½ hours, stirring occasionally.
2. Cut the marrow into 5 cm (2 inch) pieces and add them to the grams and beans. Simmer for a further 30 minutes.
3. Heat the ghee in a frying pan and fry the onion, garlic and cumin until golden brown. Remove from the heat and add the chillies and chilli powder. Transfer this mixture to a small stainless steel bowl.
4. Serve the dhal hot with the spiced onion sprinkled on top.

TOP: Pea and cream cheese pullao; BOTTOM: Gram and black bean dhal

VEGETABLES

With its large population of strict vegetarians, India has a long tradition of vegetable dishes, and has devised many unusual and ingenious ways of cooking even everyday vegetables such as peas, potatoes or cauliflower. Try Potatoes with Fenugreek, for example, to see how exotic the humble potato can be. Cooking methods vary from dry-frying, to simmering in a thick spicy sauce.

LEFT: *Stuffed aubergines;* RIGHT: *Whole potatoes*

KATHAL SHORWEDAAR
JACK FRUIT CURRY

SERVES 6
900 g (2 lb) baby jack fruit
225 g (8 oz) ghee
4 cloves
4 black peppercorns
1 black cardamom
2 green cardamoms
1 medium onion, peeled and finely chopped
4 bay leaves
6 tablespoons tomato purée
4 tablespoons plain unsweetened yogurt
1 teaspoon turmeric powder
1 teaspoon red chilli powder
300 ml (½ pint) water
salt
1 tablespoon garam masala

Paste:
1 medium onion, peeled and chopped
8 garlic cloves, crushed
15 g (½ oz) root ginger, crushed
1 tablespoon coriander seeds

Preparation time: 25 minutes
Cooking time: 1 hour
Oven: 180°C, 350°F, Gas Mark 4

Jack fruit, a relative of the bread fruit, is not always available in the markets of the West, but appears in greengrocers' shops from time to time and can also be found canned. When found and cooked, however, the dish tastes out of this world.

1. Using a greased knife and greased hands, clean the jack fruit and cut it into medium-sized pieces. Heat the ghee in a flameproof casserole and fry the fruit with the cloves, peppercorns and cardamoms until it is golden brown. Lift the fruit from the pan with a slotted spoon and set it aside.
2. Fry the onions in the ghee left in the pan until golden and add the bay leaves, tomato purée, yogurt and turmeric and chilli powders.
3. Make a fairly smooth mixture by grinding all the paste ingredients together and add this to the pan. Cook all together over a low heat until the ghee starts to separate.
4. Add the jack fruit and cook, stirring, for 5 minutes. Stir in the water, season with salt to taste and bring the mixture to the

boil. Transfer the dish to a preheated oven for about 1 hour or until the jack fruit is tender. Sprinkle with garam masala before serving.

SAAMBHAR SAUCE
SAUCE WITH VEGETABLES

2 tablespoons Saambhar masala (see page 133)
600 ml (1 pint) water
salt to taste
1 teaspoon tamarind juice
100 g (4 oz) mixed vegetables, cut into large pieces
1 tablespoon chopped fresh coriander

Preparation time: 20 minutes
Cooking time: about 20 minutes

This is the sauce normally served with dhosa and other South Indian dishes.

1. Mix the saambhar powder and water and bring to the boil. Lower the heat, stir in salt and tamarind juice and cook for another 5–7 minutes.
2. Add the vegetables and cook until they are just tender. Serve steaming hot with fresh chopped coriander sprinkled on top.

LEFT: Saambhar sauce; RIGHT: Jack fruit curry

BUNDGOBHI BHAJI
FRIED CABBAGE

100 g (4 oz) ghee
1 small onion, peeled and chopped
6 garlic cloves, crushed
1 teaspoon white cumin seeds
1 teaspoon turmeric powder
1 medium white cabbage, coarsely chopped
100 g (4 oz) potatoes, peeled and coarsely
  chopped
100 g (4 oz) shelled peas
100 g (4 oz) carrots, sliced
salt
225 g (8 oz) tomatoes, peeled and sliced
1 teaspoon green mango powder
1 green chilli, chopped
15 g (½ oz) root ginger, grated
1 teaspoon garam masala
1 tablespoon chopped coriander leaves
2 tablespoons melted butter

Preparation time: 25 minutes
Cooking time: 35 minutes

A tasty side dish which can be eaten with
puris, paraunthas or dhal and rice.

1. Melt the ghee in a saucepan and fry the
onion and garlic with the cumin until
golden brown. Add the turmeric and
shake the pan for a few seconds.
2. Add the cabbage, potatoes, peas, carrots
and salt. Cook, stirring continuously, for 5
minutes. Cover the pan and cook over a
low heat for 10 minutes.
3. Add the tomatoes, green mango
powder, chilli and ginger. Stir well, replace
the lid and continue to cook for a further
10 minutes.
4. Stir in the garam masala and chopped
coriander and heat through for 5 minutes.
Serve sprinkled with melted butter.

UPMA

SERVES 6
225 g (8 oz) semolina
1 tablespoon ghee
pinch of asafoetida powder
½ teaspoon mustard seed
4 medium potatoes, boiled, peeled and diced
1 teaspoon salt
2 green chillies, chopped
1 tablespoon mixed dhal powder
300 ml (½ pint) warm water
1 teaspoon lemon juice
2 tablespoons chopped fresh coriander
Saambhar sauce, to serve (see page 32)

Preparation time: 40 minutes
Cooking time: about 20 minutes.

1. Dry-fry the semolina on a griddle or
under a grill, making sure it does not burn.
2. Heat the ghee in a frying pan and fry the
asafoetida and mustard seed for 2
minutes.
3. Add the semolina, potatoes, salt, chillies, dhal powder and water. Cook over a
low heat for about 15 minutes, stirring
continuously. Add the lemon juice.
4. When the mixture is evenly blended
and almost dry, remove the frying pan
from the heat and sprinkle over the freshly
chopped coriander. Shape the mixture
into small balls, working quickly so as not
to burn your fingers. The Upma should be
served hot, with Saambhar sauce (see page
32).

*LEFT TO RIGHT: Fried cabbage, Upma, Saambhar
sauce (see page 32)*

PICHKI ARBI
FLATTENED ARTICHOKES

SERVES 6

675 g (1½ lb) Jerusalem artichokes
100 g (4 oz) gram flour
salt
1 teaspoon red chilli powder
1 tablespoon carom seeds
1 green chilli, chopped
vegetable oil for deep frying

Preparation time: 30 minutes
Cooking time: 15 minutes

1. Boil the artichokes in water until they are tender, about 15 minutes. Drain and peel them while they are still hot.
2. Make a batter by gradually adding water to the gram flour to make a creamy mixture. Add salt to taste with the chilli powder, carom seeds and green chilli.
3. Heat the oil to 180°C, 350°F, or until a cube of bread browns in 30 seconds. Flatten each artichoke between the palms of your hands. Dip the artichokes in the batter, 1 at a time and fry them in the oil, 2 or 3 at a time. When they are golden brown, drain them on absorbent kitchen paper and keep hot until they are all cooked. Serve hot or cold, as a dry dish with other dishes, or by themselves with bread.

BHARWAAN BAIGAN
STUFFED AUBERGINES

SERVES 6

6 small aubergines
4 tablespoons coriander seeds
2 tablespoons aniseeds
1 tablespoon white cumin seeds
1 tablespoon fenugreek seeds
1 teaspoon turmeric powder
2 green chillies, finely chopped
1 teaspoon salt
2 tablespoons lemon juice
100 g (4 oz) ghee
1 large onion, peeled and finely chopped

Preparation time: 30 minutes
Cooking time: 30 minutes

This is another variety of stuffed vegetable. In Indian cuisine, minced meat is not generally used for stuffing aubergines.

1. Clean the aubergines and slit them lengthways without halving them.
2. Roast all the spice seeds together on a baking tray. Grind them to a powder and add the turmeric. Combine this mixture with the chillies, salt and lemon juice to make a stuffing. Divide the stuffing between the aubergines and tie them with cotton to hold them together.
3. Heat the ghee in a large frying pan and fry the onion until light brown. Add the aubergines and cover the pan tightly. Leave over a low heat, turning occasionally, until the aubergines are cooked, about 20–30 minutes.

LEFT: Flattened artichokes; RIGHT: Stuffed aubergines

METHI ALOO BHAJI
FENUGREEK LEAVES AND POTATOES

4 tablespoons ghee or mustard oil
4 garlic cloves, crushed
2 dry red chillies, crushed
225 g (8 oz) fenugreek leaves, chopped
450 g (1 lb) new potatoes, quartered
2 green chillies, chopped
salt

Preparation time: 20 minutes
Cooking time: 30 minutes

This can be eaten with puris or paraunthas or served as a side dish.

1. Heat the ghee or mustard oil in a frying pan and fry the garlic until golden. Add the red chillies and cook for a few seconds.
2. Stir in the fenugreek, potato, green chillies and salt to taste. Cook over a low heat, stirring continuously, for 2–3 minutes.
3. Cover the pan tightly and cook the potatoes for about 20 minutes, until they are cooked but not beginning to break up. Shake the pan occasionally to prevent them sticking. Serve hot.

MATAR PANEER
CREAM CHEESE AND PEA CURRY

2 medium onions, chopped
6 garlic cloves, crushed
1 tablespoon coriander seeds
100 g (4 oz) ghee
225 g (8 oz) paneer (see page 138)
15 g (½ oz) root ginger, grated
4 bay leaves
1 teaspoon turmeric powder
450 g (1 lb) peas, shelled
1 × 142 ml (5 fl oz) carton plain
  unsweetened yogurt
2 green chillies, chopped
225 g (8 oz) tomatoes, peeled and sliced
salt
450 ml (¾ pint) water

To garnish:
garam masala
2 tablespoons chopped coriander leaves

Preparation time: 20 minutes
Cooking time: 45 minutes

Although this is a speciality of the Punjab region, it is cooked universally. This is a light dish which truly enhances a meatless meal. Serve with any bread or rice dishes.

1. Make a paste by grinding together half the onions, the garlic and coriander seeds.
2. Heat the ghee in a frying pan and cut the paneer into 2.5 cm (1 inch) cubes. Fry the paneer to a light brown and remove to drain on a plate.
3. Add the remaining onion and the ginger to the ghee in the pan. Add the bay leaves and fry until the onion is golden brown. Add the turmeric and the paste mixture and fry until the ghee starts to separate.
4. Add the paneer and peas along with the yogurt, chillies, tomatoes and salt. Stir for 5–6 minutes over a low heat. Pour in the water and simmer gently for 20 minutes. Serve sprinkled with garam masala and chopped coriander.

LEFT: Fenugreek leaves and potatoes; RIGHT: Cream cheese and pea curry

DUM ALOO
WHOLE POTATOES

SERVES 6

1 kg (2 lb) round new potatoes
900 ml (1½ pints) water
2 teaspoons salt
ghee or vegetable oil for deep frying
225 g (8 oz) ghee
1 large onion, peeled and finely chopped
4 tablespoons tomato purée
1 × 142 ml (5 fl oz) carton plain
  unsweetened yogurt
4 tablespoons hot water
1 green pepper, seeds removed and sliced
1 teaspoon garam masala

Spices:
4 cloves
4 bay leaves
6 black peppercorns
4 green cardamoms
1 black cardamom
1 × 5 cm (2 inch) piece cinnamon stick

Paste:
1 large onion, peeled and chopped
12 garlic cloves, crushed
25 g (1 oz) root ginger, crushed
6 black peppercorns
4 cloves
1 × 5 cm (2 inch) piece cinnamon stick
1 black cardamom
1 teaspoon poppy seeds
1 tablespoon coriander seeds
1 teaspoon black cumin seeds
2 dried red chillies
1 teaspoon turmeric powder
pinch of ground mace
pinch of grated nutmeg

Preparation time: 2½ hours
Cooking time: 1 hour
Oven: 180°C, 350°F, Gas Mark 4

1. Scrape the potatoes, prick them all over with a fork and soak them in the water with 1 teaspoon salt for 2 hours.
2. Drain the potatoes and dry them on a cloth. Heat the ghee or vegetable oil to 180°C, 350°F, or until a cube of bread browns in 30 seconds. Deep-fry the potatoes until they are golden brown. Drain them and set aside.
3. Heat the measured ghee in a flameproof casserole and fry the onion with all the spices until golden.
4. Grind the paste ingredients to a fairly smooth texture and stir into the onion. Cook for 10 minutes. Stir in the tomato purée, yogurt and remaining salt.
5. Add the potatoes and hot water and stir over a low heat for 5 minutes. Sprinkle with the pepper and garam masala and transfer the casserole to a preheated oven to cook for 20 minutes.

LEFT: Whole potatoes

KHATTI GOBHI RASEDAAR
CAULIFLOWER CURRY WITH YOGURT

SERVES 6
100 g (4 oz) ghee
pinch of asafoetida powder
675 g (1½ lb) cauliflower, cut into florets
2 × 142 ml (5 fl oz) cartons plain
  unsweetened yogurt
2 large onions, peeled and finely chopped
2 garlic cloves, crushed
salt
4 bay leaves
300 ml (½ pint) hot water

Spices:
6 cloves
6 black peppercorns
1 black cardamom
2 green cardamoms
2 × 2.5 cm (1 inch) pieces cinnamon stick
1 teaspoon coriander seeds
1 teaspoon white cumin seeds
1 teaspoon red chilli powder

To garnish:
2 tablespoons chopped coriander leaves

Preparation time: 15 minutes
Cooking time: 40 minutes

1. Heat 25 g (1 oz) ghee in a saucepan with the asafoetida. Add the cauliflower and cook over medium heat for 5 minutes. Using a slotted spoon, transfer the cauliflower to a bowl and pour over the yogurt.
2. Add the remaining ghee to the pan. When it is hot, fry the onions, garlic, salt to taste, bay leaves and all the spices except the chilli powder until golden. Stir in the chilli powder.
3. Return the cauliflower and yogurt to the pan and stir gently to combine all the ingredients. Cook over a low heat for 10 minutes.
4. Add the hot water and simmer, stirring occasionally, for 25 minutes or until the cauliflower is tender. Serve sprinkled with chopped coriander.

BAIGAN BHURTA
AUBERGINE MASH

1 large aubergine
salt
15 g (½ oz) root ginger, peeled and grated
2 green chillies, chopped
100 g (4 oz) ghee
1 large onion, peeled and chopped
6 garlic cloves, crushed
4 tablespoons chopped coriander leaves

Preparation time: 15 minutes
Cooking time: 20 minutes

Do not compare this to the sort of mashed potato dish found in the West. It is a lot more exotic, pungent and refreshingly different!

1. Boil the aubergine in sufficient water to cover for 10–15 minutes. Allow it to cool then remove the skin. Mash the aubergine flesh to a pulp and add salt to taste, the ginger and chillies.
2. Heat the ghee in a frying pan and fry the onions and garlic until golden. Add the aubergine pulp and mix well. Cook, stirring continuously, for 10–15 minutes until the mixture is well amalgamated. Serve sprinkled with the chopped coriander as a dry dish.

TOP: Cauliflower curry with yogurt; BOTTOM: Aubergine mash

MATAR KEEMA
MINCED PEAS

100 g (4 oz) ghee
1 teaspoon grated root ginger
275 g (10 oz) peas, coarsely ground
2 medium potatoes, peeled and finely
  chopped
2 bay leaves
2 onions, peeled and chopped
2 medium tomatoes, peeled and halved
2 teaspoons salt
1 tablespoon chopped coriander leaves
1½ teaspoons garam masala

Paste:
6 garlic cloves, crushed
15 g (½ oz) root ginger, grated
1½ teaspoons turmeric powder
1½ teaspoons red chilli powder
1½ teaspoons coriander seeds

Preparation time: 20 minutes
Cooking time: 30 minutes

I am sure this vegetarian dish will find favour with non-vegetarians too. It is a moist and exquisite dish – a great favourite of mine. Serve it with a rice pullao or one of the breads. Raita, pickles or chutney would be its usual accompaniments.

1. Grind all the paste ingredients together to make a smooth mixture.
2. Heat 1 tablespoon of the ghee in a frying pan over a low heat. Add the ginger and peas. Fry gently for 5 minutes until the grains of the peas start to separate. Remove and set aside. Add another tablespoon of the ghee to the pan and fry the potatoes for 5 minutes. Add them to the peas.
3. Heat the remaining ghee, add the bay leaves and onions and fry until golden brown. Reduce the heat and stir in the tomatoes and paste. Cook for 10 minutes, stirring occasionally. When the ghee starts to separate, add the pea and potato mixture with the salt. Cook, stirring, for 5 minutes.
4. Add 300 ml (½ pint) water, cover the pan and simmer for 15 minutes. Serve sprinkled with the chopped coriander and garam masala.

SAAG-PAHETA
SPINACH IN SKINLESS BLACK BEANS

SERVES 6
900 ml (1½ pints) water
salt
225 g (8 oz) skinless dried black beans
½ teaspoon turmeric powder
450 g (1 lb) spinach, coarsely chopped
15 g (½ oz) root ginger, grated
2 dry red chillies
100 g (4 oz) ghee
1 medium onion, peeled and chopped
10 garlic cloves, crushed
1 teaspoon white cumin seeds
50 g (2 oz) butter

Preparation time: 15 minutes
Cooking time: 1¾ hours

This dish gives body and muscle to a dhal mixture.

1. Boil the water in a saucepan and add the salt, beans and turmeric. Simmer, stirring occasionally, for 1 hour.
2. Add the spinach, ginger and red chillies and cook for a further 30 minutes.
3. Heat the ghee in a frying pan and fry the onion, garlic and cumin seeds until they are golden brown. Pour over the beans and spinach mixture and cook together for 10 minutes. Transfer to individual serving dishes. To serve, melt the butter and pour a little over each helping.

LEFT: Minced peas; RIGHT: Spinach in skinless black beans

PANEER KOFTE
CREAM CHEESE KOFTA CURRY

SERVES 6

900 g (2 lb) potatoes, quartered
150 ml (¼ pint) water
1 large green chilli, chopped
1 teaspoon peeled and grated root ginger
½ teaspoon garam masala
salt, to taste
2 tablespoons gram flour
2 tablespoons fresh breadcrumbs
1 tablespoon coriander seeds, roasted and
  ground
225 g (8 oz) paneer (see page 138)
1 tablespoon grated coconut
1 egg white, beaten
175 g (6 oz) ghee
2 bay leaves
2 medium onions, chopped
6 garlic cloves, crushed
4 cloves
1 black cardamom
6 black peppercorns
1 × 142 ml (5 fl oz) carton plain
  unsweetened yogurt
1 teaspoon turmeric powder
1 teaspoon red chilli powder
300 ml (½ pint) water

Topping:
450 g (1 lb) tomatoes, peeled and sliced
½ teaspoon garam masala
2 tablespoons chopped coriander leaves

Preparation time: 30 minutes
Cooking time: 1 hour
Oven: 180°C, 350°F, Gas Mark 4

1. Boil the potatoes in the water with the green chilli, ginger and all but a pinch of the garam masala. When tender, drain and mash thoroughly with the salt, gram flour, breadcrumbs and coriander. Divide into 12 equal portions.
2. Mix the paneer with the coconut and the remaining garam masala. Divide this mixture into 12 equal portions. Flatten each portion of potato and use to wrap 1 portion of paneer. Roll into balls and brush with the beaten egg white.
3. Heat the ghee and fry the balls until light golden brown all over. Drain and arrange the balls in a casserole dish.
4. Add the bay leaves, onion, garlic, cloves, cardamom and peppercorns to the ghee left in the pan. Fry until the onion is golden brown. Add the yogurt and the turmeric and chilli powders. Mix well, pour in the water and bring to the boil. Simmer for 10 minutes.
5. Pour this sauce over the koftas, cover with the tomato, garam masala and coriander leaves and cook in a preheated oven for 10–15 minutes, or until heated through.

DAIRY PRODUCTS

It is not immediately obvious to westerners, whose chief experience of Indian food comes from the occasional meal in a restaurant, that dairy products are a crucial element in the Indian diet all over the sub-continent. This is partly because our ideas of dairy products focus on the way milk, cream, butter and cheese are used in European cookery, in rich sauces, soups, gratin dishes, nursery puddings and the like; and partly because it is the magical use of spices that has most impressed and entranced the western palate.

Ghee (clarified butter), milk and curds, however, formed three of the seven oceans which, according to the ancient writings, encircled Mount Meru – the centre of the human world. Such was their importance, and still today ghee, yogurt, milk and other by-products such as paneer (see page 138) are essential items in Indian cooking. It is this as much as other religious reasons (such as the belief in the transmigration of souls) that has made the cow a sacred animal in India.

LEFT: Cream cheese kofta curry

NAWRATAN TARKARI
COCKTAIL CURRY

50g (2 oz) butter
1 onion, chopped
1 teaspoon white cumin seeds
225 g (8 oz) potatoes, cubed
1 small cauliflower, cut in florets
1 small aubergine, peeled and coarsely
  chopped
100g (4 oz) shelled peas
450 g (1 lb) tomatoes, peeled and quartered
100 g (4 oz) carrots, chopped
1 small turnip, chopped
1 small bunch spring onions, chopped
100 g (4 oz) marrow flesh, chopped
1 × 142 ml (5 fl oz) carton plain
  unsweetened yogurt
150 ml (¼ pint) water
salt
2 green chillies, finely chopped
1 teaspoon garam masala

To garnish:
1 tablespoon chopped coriander leaves

Preparation time: 35 minutes
Cooking time: 40 minutes

This is the choicest vegetable curry. It caters for all vegetarian preferences as the specified vegetables can, of course, be altered or substituted. The famous South Indian dish, Aviyal, is made in the same way, by simply mashing the flesh of a coconut to a purée with the milk from the shell and adding it to the mixture with the green chillies.

1. Heat the butter in a saucepan and fry the onion with the cumin until golden brown. Stir in all the prepared vegetables and cook, stirring, for 5 minutes.
2. Mix the yogurt and water together and stir into the curry. Add the salt, green chillies and garam masala and cook, stirring, for 2–3 minutes. Cover and simmer gently for 30 minutes. Serve hot, garnished with the chopped coriander.

BHINDI BHAJI
FRIED OKRA

100 g (4 oz) ghee or mustard oil
6 garlic cloves, crushed
1 teaspoon turmeric powder
2 dried red chillies, crushed
1 teaspoon white cumin seeds
450 g (1 lb) okra, sliced
2 green chillies, chopped
15 g (½ oz) root ginger, grated
salt
1 tablespoon green mango powder
1 tablespoon butter

Preparation time: 10 minutes
Cooking time: 35 minutes

A delicious bhaji – eat it with paraunthas or rice and dhal. Bhindis are also known as ladyfingers.

1. Heat the ghee or mustard oil in a frying pan and fry the garlic until light brown. Remove from the heat and add the turmeric, red chillies and cumin seeds. Stir well and return to the heat.
2. Add the okra, chillies and ginger and mix well. Cook, uncovered, for 20 minutes, stirring occasionally.
3. When the okra is cooked, add salt to taste with the green mango powder and

cook for a further 5–10 minutes. Serve dotted with the butter.

TOP: Cocktail curry (2 versions); BOTTOM: Fried okra

LAUKI KOFTE
MARROW KOFTA CURRY

450 g (1 lb) marrow flesh
4 tablespoons gram flour
2 teaspoons garam masala
salt
15 g (½ oz) root ginger, grated
2 green chillies, finely chopped
225 g (8 oz) ghee
2 medium onions, peeled and finely chopped
2 bay leaves
1 black cardamom
4 cloves
225 g (8 oz) tomatoes, peeled and sliced
300 ml (½ pint) water

Paste:
1 medium onion, peeled and chopped
4 garlic cloves, crushed
1 teaspoon white cumin seeds
1 teaspoon turmeric powder

Preparation time: 1½ hours
Cooking time: 45 minutes

1. Grate the marrow and mix with the gram flour, 1 teaspoon of the garam masala, about 1 teaspoon salt, the ginger and green chillies. Form the mixture into small balls. Chill on absorbent kitchen paper for 2 hours.
2. Heat the ghee in a saucepan and fry the balls until they are golden brown. Drain and set aside.
3. Add the onions to the ghee remaining in the pan with the bay leaves, cardamom and cloves. Fry until the onion is golden brown.
4. Grind the paste ingredients together until fairly smooth then add to the onion mixture and cook for 5–7 minutes, stirring occasionally until the ghee starts to separate.
5. Stir in the tomatoes and salt to taste and mix in the water. Drop in the fried marrow balls and heat them through gently in the sauce. Sprinkle with the remaining garam masala 5 minutes before serving.

TORAI DO-PIAZZA
COURGETTE AND ONION

1 kg (2 lb) courgettes, trimmed and peeled
2 tablespoons ghee
450 g (1 lb) large onions, peeled and thinly sliced
2 garlic cloves, crushed
1 green chilli, chopped or 1 teaspoon red chilli powder
1½ teaspoons salt

Preparation time: 10 minutes
Cooking time: 25 minutes

LEFT: Marrow kofta curry; RIGHT: Courgette and onion

This dish is moist when cooked and is delicious eaten with any of the breads. It can also be eaten with a rice dish, provided that it is accompanied by a curry.

1. Cut the courgettes into 2.5 cm (1 inch) pieces. Heat the ghee in a saucepan over a moderate heat. Add half the onions and the garlic and fry until light brown.
2. Mix in the chilli or chilli powder and cook for a few minutes, stirring. Add the salt and courgettes and cook for about 5 minutes, stirring continuously.
3. Add the remaining onions and stir well.

Reduce the heat, cover and leave to simmer for about 15 minutes or until the onions are soft and tender. Serve hot with puris or paraunthas.

GOBHI-ALOO-MATAR
CAULIFLOWER, POTATO AND PEA CURRY

100 g (4 oz) ghee
pinch of asafoetida powder
1 small cauliflower, cut in florets
450 g (1 lb) potatoes, quartered
100 g (4 oz) shelled peas
1 medium onion, finely chopped
2 cloves
1 teaspoon white cumin seeds
1 black cardamom
450 g (1 lb) tomatoes, peeled and thinly
  sliced
450 ml (¾ pint) water
salt to taste

Paste:
1 medium onion, chopped
4 garlic cloves, crushed
1 × 2.5 cm (1 inch) piece root ginger,
  crushed
1 teaspoon turmeric powder
1 teaspoon red chilli powder
1 tablespoon roasted coriander seeds
½ teaspoon ground cinnamon

To garnish:
1 teaspoon garam masala
2 tablespoons chopped coriander leaves

Preparation time: 15 minutes
Cooking time: 1 hour

This combination of vegetables makes a delicious curry. Experiment with alternative vegetables too.

1. Heat 25 g (1 oz) ghee in a saucepan and add the asafoetida powder. Stir for 5 seconds then add the cauliflower, potatoes and peas. Fry for 5 minutes over a moderate heat. Remove the vegetables to a plate and set aside.
2. Heat the remaining ghee and add the onion, cloves, cumin and cardamom and fry until the onion is golden brown.
3. Make a fairly smooth mixture by grinding all the paste ingredients together. Add the paste to the onion mixture and cook until the ghee starts to separate.
4. Mix in the fried vegetables and tomatoes and fry for 5 minutes, stirring occasionally. Stir in the water and salt and simmer for 30 minutes. Serve hot, garnished with the garam masala and chopped coriander.

RIGHT: Cauliflower, potato and pea curry

FISH

Living in a country with an extensive coastline, large lakes and enormous rivers, Indians have access to a wide variety of fish, with more than 2000 varieties to choose from. The Indian coastal regions, particularly Bengal, Malabar and Goa, are noted for their wonderful fish and seafood dishes. Impress your guests with the deliciously flavoured Fish in Coconut Milk, or exotic Stuffed Crabs.

TOP: *Fish in coconut milk*; BOTTOM: *Lobster curry*

BATAKH-MACHHLI KI TIKKI
BOMBAY DUCK NUGGETS

10 Bombay ducks, canned
225 g (8 oz) mashed potato
½ teaspoon red chilli powder
1 green chilli, finely chopped
1 teaspoon garam masala
1 teaspoon salt
1 medium onion, finely chopped

Batter:
225 g (½ lb) gram flour
300 ml (½ pint) water
oil for deep frying

To Serve:
tomato sauce

Preparation time: 20 minutes
Cooking time: 15 minutes

Bombay duck is a fish, the size of a herring, found on the west coast of India, mainly around Bombay. It has the unfishlike wont of swimming on the surface of the water, rather like a duck.

When raw, this fish smells foul – much more so than other fishes – but when cooked, it smells pleasant and tastes super. It is prepared in many different ways but is usually soaked, cleaned, cut and cured first. In the West it is available in cans. The fish can be baked in the oven and crumbled over a rice dish, fried in fat, or mixed with other ingredients and converted into chops, cutlets or kebabs. The recipe can be eaten as a teatime savoury or as a side dish with the main meal.

1. Break the Bombay ducks into small pieces. Mix the potato, chilli powder, green chilli, garam masala, salt and onion and combine together thoroughly. Divide this mixture into 8 portions and form into small bullet shapes.
2. Combine the batter ingredients to make a smooth mixture. Heat the oil in a deeppan to 180°C, 350°F or until a cube of bread browns in 30 seconds. Dip the bullets into the batter, one at a time, and deep fry in the oil until golden brown. Serve hot with tomato sauce.

TALI MACHHLI
FRIED FISH

SERVES 6
1 kg (2 lb) white fish fillets, e.g. cod,
  haddock or halibut
½ teaspoon turmeric powder
salt
100 g (4 oz) gram flour
450 ml (¾ pint) water
½ teaspoon red chilli powder
½ teaspoon ground black pepper
2 tablespoons chopped coriander leaves
1 green chilli, chopped
vegetable oil for deep frying

To garnish:
2 tomatoes, sliced
1 lemon, sliced

Preparation time: 30 minutes
Cooking time: 20 minutes

1. Wash the fish and cut it into convenient-sized pieces. Rub the turmeric over the pieces with about 1 teaspoon salt and set them aside for 10–15 minutes. Rinse the fish under cold running water.
2. Combine the gram flour and breadcrumbs with 450 ml (¾ pint) water, beating well to make a smooth batter. Beat in the salt, chilli powder, black pepper, coriander and green chilli.
3. Heat the oil to 180°C, 350°F, or until a cube of bread will brown in 30 seconds. Pat the fish pieces dry with kitchen paper. Dip the fish pieces in batter to coat them evenly and deep-fry them until they are golden all over, about 7-10 minutes. Serve hot, garnished with slices of tomato and lemon.

LEFT: Fried fish; RIGHT: Bombay duck nuggets

SAMUCHE KEKDE
STUFFED CRABS

SERVES 6

6 small crabs, cooked
50 g (2 oz) ghee
1 large onion, peeled and finely chopped
2 cloves garlic, peeled and crushed
2 green chillies, chopped
½ teaspoon grated fresh ginger
1 slice of bread, soaked in water
1 teaspoon cornflour
1 teaspoon garam masala
½ teaspoon turmeric
1 tablespoon lemon juice
salt
onion rings
tomato slices

Preparation time: 1 hour
Cooking time: 15 minutes

1. Remove the flesh from the crabs (see right). Flake the flesh. Wash the shells thoroughly with clear water and wipe them dry, inside and out.
2. Heat the ghee in a frying pan and fry the onion until golden. Add the remaining ingredients and the crab flesh. Fry over moderate heat until the mixture is dry. Remove the pan from the heat and allow it to cool a little.
3. Pack the mixture into the cleaned crab shells. Place under a hot grill for 5 minutes or until the tops begin to brown. Serve immediately with a garnish of onion rings and tomato slices.

JHEENGA SHORWEDAAR
PRAWN CURRY

4 tablespoons ghee
1 large onion, peeled and finely chopped
3 tablespoons coconut flour
15 g (½ oz) root ginger, grated
2 green chillies, chopped
5 cloves
5 green cardamoms
5 bay leaves
½ teaspoon black cumin seeds
1 teaspoon turmeric powder
½ teaspoon red chilli powder
salt
1 teaspoon sugar
2 tablespoons plain unsweetened yogurt
1.2 litres (2 pints) prawns, peeled
300 ml (½ pint) water

Preparation time: 15 minutes
Cooking time: 40 minutes

A rather expensive delicacy by Indian standards and a great favourite with fish lovers.

1. Heat the ghee in a saucepan and fry the onion until it is golden brown. Drain the onion and set it aside to keep warm.
2. Add the coconut flour, ginger and green chillies to the ghee remaining in the pan, together with all the spices. Fry gently for 2–3 minutes. Stir in the salt, sugar and yogurt and continue to cook for a further 2–3 minutes.
3. Stir in the prawns. Cook over a low heat for 5 minutes, stirring continuously. Add the water, cover and leave the curry to simmer for 10 minutes. Serve hot, sprinkled with the hot fried onion.

TOP: Stuffed crabs; BOTTOM: Prawn curry

DUM KADDU MACHHLI
BAKED SQUID

1 squid, about 450 g (1 lb)
salt to taste
1 teaspoon red chilli powder
¼ teaspoon green cardamom powder
pinch of garam masala
lemon juice as necessary
ghee as necessary
½ teaspoon cumin powder
½ teaspoon ground coriander
½ teaspoon mango powder
1 green chilli, chopped
1 tablespoon chopped coriander leaves
1 large potato boiled, peeled and mashed
1 tablespoon peas
2 tablespoons grated fresh coconut
butter, for greasing
vegetable oil

Preparation time: 1 hour
Cooking time: 1 hour

1. Pull the head and tentacles away from the body and cut off the tentacles just below the eyes. Clean the squid, pulling off the thin membrane, and scrub the tentacles. Slash the thickest part of the tentacles to help it cook through.
2. Mix ½ teaspoon salt, half the chilli powder, all the cardamom powder and garam masala and enough lemon juice to make a thin paste. Brush this paste all over the squid – inside and out.
3. Heat 1 tablespoon ghee in a frying pan and fry the cumin, coriander, mango powder, chilli, potato, peas and coconut, with the rest of the chilli powder and salt to taste, over a moderate heat for about 5 minutes. Remove from the heat and leave to cool a little.
4. Stuff this mixture inside the squid and replace the tentacles to reform the squid

shape. Place on a greased baking tray and sprinkle with cooking oil. Place in a preheated moderate oven (160°C, 325°F, Gas Mark 3) and bake for about 1 hour until cooked.

RASEDAAR LUBDER
LOBSTER CURRY

2 tablespoons ghee
1 medium onion, chopped
4 garlic cloves, peeled and finely chopped
½ teaspoon grated fresh ginger root
2 green chillies, chopped
1 teaspoon chopped curry leaves
4 medium potatoes, peeled and quartered
salt
150 ml (¼ pint) coconut milk
½ teaspoon red chilli powder
4 small lobsters, claws cracked and shells
  cracked
2 tablespoons chopped coriander leaves
½ teaspoon garam masala

Preparation time: 1 hour
Cooking time: 25 minutes

1. Heat the ghee in a frying pan and fry the onion, garlic, ginger, chillies and curry leaves over a moderate heat for 2 minutes.
2. Add the potatoes with salt to taste, and fry for 5 minutes gently. Pour in the coconut milk and add the chilli powder. Lower the heat, cover and cook for about 15 minutes until softened.
3. When the potatoes are soft add the lobsters, cut up, and cook for a further 5-10 miniutes until heated through. Sprinkle with the coriander leaves and garam masala and serve hot.

LEFT: Baked squid; RIGHT: Lobster curry

MACHHLI MASAALEDAAR
BENGALI FISH CURRY

SERVES 6
750 g (1½ lb) white fish fillet, e.g. cod,
  haddock or halibut
100 g (4 oz) ghee
2 medium onions, peeled
1 teaspoon white cumin seeds
1 teaspoon turmeric powder
1 teaspoon garam masala
4 garlic cloves, crushed
15 g (½ oz) root ginger, crushed
4 tablespoons tomato purée
salt
6 tomatoes, peeled and halved

Preparation time: 15 minutes
Cooking time: 20 minutes

A dish in great demand in the riparian restaurants. Bengalis are crazy about fish and are known for their excellent fish dishes.

1. Cut the fish into medium-sized pieces. Heat the ghee in a frying pan and fry the fish gently for 5 minutes. Drain the fish on absorbent kitchen paper and set aside.
2. Chop one onion finely and grind the other one. Add the chopped onion to the ghee in the pan and fry until golden brown. Add the cumin seeds, turmeric and garam masala and cook, stirring, for about 10 seconds. Add the ground onion, garlic, ginger and tomato purée and fry the mixture until the ghee starts to separate.
3. Pour in 150 ml (¼ pint) water and add salt to taste. Bring the mixture to the boil, remove from the heat and add the fried fish. Return to a low heat and simmer for 10 minutes.
4. Transfer the curry to a heated dish and serve, garnished with tomato halves.

BHARWAAN MACHHLI
STUFFED HERRINGS

50 g (2 oz) butter
1 large onion, peeled and chopped
1 teaspoon white cumin seeds
1 teaspoon grated root ginger
salt
2 green chillies, finely chopped
1 tablespoon chopped coriander leaves
1 tablespoon lemon juice
450 g (1 lb) potatoes, peeled, boiled and
  crushed
1 teaspoon vinegar
4 medium herrings, cleaned and gutted
75 g (3 oz) gram flour
1 tablespoon fresh breadcrumbs
vegetable oil for deep frying
4 lettuce hearts
1 lemon, sliced
1 tablespoon chopped coriander leaves

Preparation time: 20 minutes
Cooking time: 20 minutes

Serve as a side dish with a non-vegetarian meal for a special occasion.

1. Heat the butter in a frying pan and fry the onion until golden. Add the cumin seeds, ginger, salt, green chillies and chopped coriander. Mix together with the lemon juice, crushed potato and vinegar.
2. Stuff the herrings with the potato mixture.
3. Make a batter by beating together the gram flour with 150 ml (¼ pint) water and breadcrumbs until smooth. Dip the fish in the batter until coated all over.
4. Heat the oil to 180°C, 350°F, or until a cube of bread browns in 30 seconds. Add the fish and fry on both sides until crisp and golden.
5. Garnish with lettuce hearts, lemon slices and coriander, and serve hot.

TOP: *Bengal fish curry;* BOTTOM: *Stuffed herrings*

DOODHIA MACHHLI
FISH IN COCONUT MILK

2 cloves, ground
4 green cardamoms, ground
2 green chillies, crushed
2 cloves garlic, peeled and crushed
1 cm (½ inch) piece ginger root, peeled and
  chopped
1 tablespoon Vindaloo masala (see page
  133)
salt
lemon juice
450 g (1 lb) fish fillets (sole, plaice or other
  white fish)
2 tablespoons mustard oil
1 medium onion, peeled and thinly sliced
300 ml (½ pint) coconut milk
1 tablespoon chopped fresh coriander

Preparation time: 20 minutes
Cooking time: about 30 minutes

Salmon steaks can also be cooked in this way and would make a good party dish.

1. Mix together the cloves, cardamoms, chillies, garlic, ginger, vindaloo powder and salt to taste, with enough lemon juice to make a smooth, thick paste.
2. Wash the fillets and pat them dry with absorbent kitchen paper. Spread the paste thickly and evenly over the fish.
3. Heat the mustard oil in a large saucepan. Fry the onion until soft and golden. Add the fish pieces and fry on both sides until golden brown.
4. Pour in the coconut milk and season with salt to taste. Cover the pan and cook over moderate heat for 15 minutes. Serve the fish hot, sprinkled with chopped fresh coriander.

MACHHLI KABAB
HADDOCK CROQUETTES

450 g (1 lb) haddock fillet, steamed and
  flaked
4 slices bread, soaked in water and
  squeezed dry
1 medium onion, peeled and chopped
1 teaspoon grated root ginger
1 teaspoon garlic powder
1 tablespoon chopped coriander leaves
½ teaspoon freshly ground black pepper
2 green chillies, finely chopped
2 teaspoons salt
2 egg whites
50 g (2 oz) fresh breadcrumbs
vegetable oil for deep frying
tomato or mint sauce, to serve

Preparation time: 25 minutes
Cooking time: 20 minutes

This dish makes a marvellous light meal. It can also be served as a snack with tea or drinks. If preferred, the haddock can be replaced by cod or other white fish.

1. Mix the haddock with the soaked bread. Add the onion, ginger, garlic powder, coriander, pepper, chillies and salt and mix together to form a dough. Divide this dough into 16 portions and mould them to the required shape. Chill until firm.
2. Beat the egg whites until fluffy and dip in each croquette. Roll the croquettes in the breadcrumbs to coat them.
3. Heat the oil to 180°C, 350°F, or until a cube of bread browns in 30 seconds. Deep-fry 3 or 4 croquettes at a time until golden. Serve hot with tomato or mint sauce.

TOP: Fish in coconut milk; BOTTOM: Haddock croquettes

POULTRY

Chicken is very popular all over India, largely because of the various religious taboos associated with beef and pork. It is usually skinned and cut up before cooking, so that the spices and flavourings can permeate the food. The tandoori method of baking chicken is, perhaps, the best known, but there is a great variety of cooking methods, from the fiery vindaloo of the south, to the gentler, milder korma.

Grilled drumsticks

MURGHI BIRIYANI
CHICKEN BIRIYANI

8 chicken drumsticks
175 g (6 oz) ghee
25 g (1 oz) almonds, chopped
25 g (1 oz) cashew nuts, chopped
1 large onion, peeled and finely chopped
Biriyani spices
  4 bay leaves
450 g (1 lb) long-grain rice
½ teaspoon saffron strands
2 tablespoons butter, melted

Paste:
1 teaspoon garam masala
1 small onion, chopped
2 garlic cloves, crushed
1 × 5 cm (2 inch) piece root ginger
142 ml (5 fl oz) plain yogurt
1 teaspoon salt

Preparation time: 1 hour
Cooking time: 50 minutes

This superb dish is a gourmet's delight. If desired, duck can be substituted for chicken. Very wholesome and good for peace and quiet in the dining room!

1. Grind all the paste ingredients together to make a smooth mixture. Rub the paste over the chicken pieces and leave them for 30 minutes.
2. Heat the ghee in a frying pan and fry the almonds and cashews. When they are golden brown, lift the nuts out of the pan with a slotted spoon and leave them on absorbent kitchen paper to drain. Set them aside for a garnish. In the ghee left in the pan fry the onion until golden. Lift half the cooked onion from the pan and set it aside to garnish.
3. Add the bay leaves and Biriyani spices to the remaining onion. Shake the pan and add the chicken pieces. Cook over a mod-

erate heat for 20 minutes. Add the rice and mix well. Add 900 ml (1½ pints) warm water and salt and leave covered for 15–20 minutes over a moderate heat until the water is absorbed and the rice is tender.
4. Steep the saffron in a little warm water for 5–10 minutes. Add the melted butter and stir it into the rice mixture. Transfer to a warmed dish and serve garnished with the reserved fried onions and nuts.

BIRIYANI SPICES:
4 cloves
8 black peppercorns
4 green cardamoms
1 black cardamom, crushed
1 × 5 cm (2 inch) piece cinnamon stick
½ teaspoon turmeric powder

TANDOORI MURGHA TAANGEN
GRILLED DRUMSTICKS

1 kg (2 lb) chicken drumsticks, skin
  removed and flesh pricked with a fork
2 teaspoons salt
4 tablespoons Tandoori masala (page 133)
4 tablespoons oil
2 tablespoons lemon juice
2 medium onions, peeled and thinly sliced

To garnish:
4 lemons, sliced in rounds

Preparation time: 25 minutes
Cooking time: 30 minutes

This succulent savoury dish can be eaten as a snack or a side dish. However, it requires constant attention for perfect results.

1. Place the drumsticks on a baking sheet. Mix the salt and tandoori powder and rub half of it on one side of the drumsticks. Turn them over and use the other half on the other side. Prick the meat on the drumsticks with a fork.
2. Pour half of the oil over the drumsticks and put the baking sheet under the grill at a low heat. When the drumsticks get slightly brown, take them out, turn them over and pour the rest of the oil over them.

Return to the grill once again. When both sides are browned, continue until the chicken is cooked. Test them with a fork. If they are tender and the juices are golden (not pink) they are ready. Pour the lemon juice over the drumsticks and set aside to keep warm.
3. Pour the oil from the baking sheet into a frying pan and cook the onion rings quickly until they are golden brown. Serve the drumsticks hot on a bed of fried onion rings, garnished with slices of lemon.

TOP: Chicken biryani; BOTTOM: Grilled drumsticks

MURGHA MUSALLAM WHOLE CHICKEN

SERVES 6

1 × 2 kg (4½ lb) chicken
225 g (8 oz) ghee
2 large onions, peeled and finely chopped
2 bay leaves
4 cloves
4 green cardamoms
1 teaspoon turmeric powder
1 teaspoon red chilli powder
1 tablespoon roasted coriander
1 teaspoon black cumin seeds
25 g (1 oz) root ginger, grated
3 tablespoons plain unsweetened yogurt
225 g (8 oz) tomatoes, peeled and sliced
½ teaspoon salt
½ teaspoon saffron strands
1 teaspoon garam masala
2 tablespoons chopped parsley or coriander
   leaves

Marinade:
7 cloves garlic, crushed
15 g (½ oz) root ginger, grated
1 teaspoon garam masala
1 tablespoon salt
2 teaspoons turmeric powder
3 tablespoons plain unsweetened yogurt
1 tablespoon lemon juice

Stuffing:
225 g (8 oz) long-grain rice
100 g (4 oz) shelled peas
3 garlic cloves, crushed
4 cloves
6 black peppercorns
1 brown cardamom
4 bay leaves

LEFT: Whole chicken, served with Fried okra and Salad

Preparation time: 30 minutes plus marinating
Cooking time: 1½ hours
Oven: 200°C, 400°F, Gas Mark 6

1. Combine the marinade ingredients to make a paste. Make small cuts in the chicken flesh. Rub the paste all over the chicken and in the cavity. Leave for 2 hours.
2. Place the stuffing ingredients in a large saucepan with plenty of lightly salted water. Bring to the boil and cook until the rice is half cooked. Drain the rice mixture and stuff the chicken.
3. Heat 120 g (4½ oz) ghee in a saucepan and fry the chicken until it is brown all over, taking care not to let the stuffing spill out. Lift the chicken out of the pan, let it drain and set it aside to keep warm.
4. Heat the remaining ghee in a flame-proof casserole large enough to hold the chicken. Fry half the onion with the bay leaves, cloves and green cardamoms until golden. Add the turmeric and chilli powder.
5. Grind together the coriander, cumin seeds, ginger and remaining onion to a smooth paste and add them to the casserole. Cook, stirring, for 5–10 minutes, until the ghee starts to separate. Mix in the yogurt, tomatoes and salt.
6. Place the chicken in the casserole and baste it with the mixture. Pour over 300 ml (½ pint) hot water. Cover the casserole and transfer to a preheated oven to cook for 1 hour.
7. Steep the saffron in 150 ml (¼ pint) hot water and sprinkle it over the chicken 10 minutes before the end of the cooking time. Serve hot, sprinkled with garam masala and chopped parsley or coriander.

MURGHI DO-PIAZZA
CHICKEN WITH ONIONS

1 chicken, about 1.5 kg (3 lb)
½–1 tablespoon salt
2 tablespoons lemon juice
175 g (6 oz) ghee
6 cloves
1 brown cardamom
12 black peppercorns
2 × 2.5 cm (1 inch) pieces cinnamon stick
4 large onions, peeled and coarsely chopped
2 garlic cloves, crushed
½ teaspoon ground ginger
1 teaspoon turmeric powder
1 teaspoon red chilli powder
2 × 142 ml (5 fl oz) cartons plain
  unsweetened yogurt
300 ml (½ pint) water
1 teaspoon garam masala
225 g (8 oz) tomatoes, peeled and halved
1 medium onion, peeled, chopped and fried

Preparation time: 40 minutes
Cooking time: 1¼ hours
Oven: 180°C, 350°F, Gas Mark 4

This dish pleases those who like a preponderance of onions – adapt the quantity of onion to your liking.

1. Cut the chicken into 4 or 8 pieces. Mix the salt with the lemon juice and rub it all over the chicken. Leave the chicken to marinate for 30 minutes.
2. Heat the ghee in a flameproof casserole and add the cloves, cardamom, peppercorns and cinnamon. Stir well then add the chicken, onions, garlic, ginger, turmeric and chilli powder. Cook gently for 15 minutes, stirring continuously.
3. Add the yogurt and stir for 5 minutes

over a low heat. Add the water, cover and simmer for 40–50 minutes, or until the chicken is tender.
4. Sprinkle the top with garam masala. Arrange the tomato halves around the dish and cover with the onion. Cook in a preheated oven for 10 minutes before serving.

MURGHA KORMA
CHICKEN KORMA

175 g (6 oz) ghee
2 medium onions, peeled and finely chopped
Korma spice mixture
6 garlic cloves, crushed
4 tablespoons plain unsweetened yogurt
2 bay leaves
salt
4 chicken portions
225 g (8 oz) tomatoes, peeled and sliced
1 tablespoon lemon juice

Preparation time: 20 minutes
Cooking time: 50 minutes

This is a recipe for a genuine korma, as cooked in the Nawabs' courts. For variety add ½ teaspoon saffron strands steeped in a little hot water just before serving, or add cashew nuts or almonds with the sliced tomatoes.

1. Heat the ghee in a saucepan and fry the onions until they are golden brown. Set aside half the cooked onion. Add all the Korma spice mixture except the garam masala to the onion left in the pan, along with the garlic, yogurt and bay leaves. Season with salt to taste. Stir over a low heat for 5 minutes.

2. Add the chicken portions to the pan and cook them gently for 5 minutes. Add the tomatoes, lemon juice and garam masala and stir well. Still stirring, pour in the water. Cover the pan and simmer for 30-40 minutes, or until tender.

KORMA SPICE MIXTURE:
4 cloves
8 black peppercorns
2 × 2.5 cm (1 inch) pieces cinnamon stick
1 teaspoon black cardamom seeds
1 teaspoon black cumin seeds
1 teaspoon ground ginger
1 teaspoon red chilli powder
1 teaspoon garam masala
1 teaspoon turmeric powder

TOP: Chicken with onions; BOTTOM: Chicken korma

TANDOORI MURGHA
TANDOORI CHICKEN

SERVES 6

1 × 1.5 kg (3 lb) chicken, skin removed
2 teaspoons salt
2 tablespoons lemon juice
4 tablespoons ghee
½ teaspoon saffron strands

Paste:
4 red chillies
1½ teaspoons turmeric powder
2 tablespoons coriander seeds
2 teaspoons garam masala
6 garlic cloves, crushed
1 medium onion, peeled and coarsely
  chopped
15 g (½ oz) root ginger, grated

To garnish:
4 lemons, sliced in rounds
1 medium onion, peeled and sliced in rings

Preparation time: 30 minutes
Cooking time: 1 hour
Oven: 200°C, 400°F, Gas Mark 6

Tandoori cooking is the culmination of the Indian culinary art. It was originally a Punjabi way of cooking food, now adopted and prevalent worldwide. Tandoori chicken is one of the most famous of all Indian dishes. It is economical and easy to make and has a taste and deliciousness which defy description. An excellent dish which can be served with one of the Indian breads such as a naan or with a rice pullao.

1. Grind all the paste ingredients together to make a smooth mixture. Steam the chicken over hot water for about 10 minutes. Drain off the water, place the chicken on a platter, prick it all over with a fork. Mix the salt and lemon juice into the paste and rub it all over the chicken and inside the cavity. Leave it to permeate the flesh for about 10 minutes.
2. Warm the ghee in a large saucepan over a low heat. Sprinkle the saffron over it and carefully lower the chicken into the pan. Cook, turning it over occasionally, for about 10 minutes.
3. Transfer the chicken and pan juices to a lidded casserole and bake in a preheated oven for 30 minutes, or until the chicken is tender. Serve hot, garnished with slices of lemon and onion rings.

TANDOOR COOKING

A tandoor oven is made of clay, shaped like a barrel, and fuelled with charcoal or wood. Pieces of meat to be cooked in it must first be marinated to keep them tender and succulent. They are then placed on a skewer and inserted vertically into the oven where they cook very quickly in the fierce, dry heat. The sides of the oven are sometimes used to cook bread, and other dishes may be baked in the ashes at the bottom. To cook chicken in the tandoori style but in a conventional oven it is important to remove the skin and helpful to joint it if it is very large. The flesh must be marinated with a traditional blend of spices. The marinating time may be brief, but can be extended all day or overnight. Be sure the oven is preheated to the required temperature.

LEFT: Tandoori chicken

MURGHI VINDALOO
CHICKEN VINDALOO

SERVES 6

2 tablespoons Vindaloo masala (see page 133)

2 teaspoons vinegar

salt

1 × 1.5 kg (3 lb) chicken, cut in pieces

6 tablespoons mustard oil

4 bay leaves

1 teaspoon green cardamom seeds

1 large onion, peeled and thinly sliced

2 teaspoons turmeric powder

1 teaspoon cayenne

10 garlic cloves, crushed

15 g (½ oz) root ginger, thinly sliced

2 medium tomatoes, peeled and quartered

150 ml (¼ pint) tamarind juice

2 teaspoons desiccated coconut

Preparation time: 1½ hours
Cooking time: 55 minutes

Vindaloo is a delicacy brought to perfection by the southern Indians and also the Goanese. It is usually made very hot and sour. It is the hottest curry of south India where even the mild curries are hotter than the hot curries elsewhere.

1. Combine the Vindaloo masala, vinegar and 2 teaspoons salt to make a smooth paste. Make a few deep gashes on the chicken pieces and rub the paste over them. Leave to marinate for 1 hour.
2. Heat the mustard oil in a saucepan over a moderate heat. Stir in the bay leaves and cardamom seeds, then add the onion and fry until light brown. Add the turmeric and cayenne, stir well and add the chicken pieces. Continue to cook, stirring, for about 15 minutes.
3. Add 1 teaspoon salt, garlic, ginger and tomatoes to the pan and cook for a further 10 minutes, still stirring.
4. When the fat starts separating, add the tamarind juice together with the water. Stir once or twice. Cover with a tightly fitting lid, reduce the heat and leave to simmer for about 25 minutes until the chicken is tender. Garnish with the desiccated coconut and serve hot.

RASEDAAR MURGHI TAANGEN
CHICKEN CURRY

100 g (4 oz) ghee

2 medium onions, peeled and finely chopped

4 garlic cloves, crushed

4 cloves

1 × 5 cm (2 inch) piece cinnamon stick

4 black peppercorns

1 brown cardamom

2 green cardamoms

2 tablespoons tomato purée

15 g (½ oz) root ginger, chopped

1 tablespoon lemon juice

8 chicken drumsticks

1 teaspoon turmeric powder

1 teaspoon red chilli powder

4 tablespoons plain unsweetened yogurt

salt

1 teaspoon garam masala

1 tablespoon chopped parsley or coriander leaves

Preparation time: 15 minutes
Cooking time: 50 minutes

1. Heat the ghee in a saucepan and fry the onion, garlic, cloves, cinnamon, peppercorns, and cardamoms until they are golden brown.
2. Add the tomato purée, ginger, lemon juice, chicken drumsticks, and turmeric and chilli powders. Mix well and cook for 15 minutes over a low heat.
3. Combine the yogurt with 300 ml (½ pint) hot water and salt and stir into the chicken mixture. Bring to the boil, cover and simmer for about 30 minutes or until the chicken is tender. Sprinkle with garam masala and parsley or coriander before serving.

TOP: *Chicken vindaloo*; BOTTOM: *chicken curry*

MEAT

The most usual red meat eaten in India is goat, or lamb. Because of religious taboos, beef or pork dishes tend to be highly regional. As with poultry, meat is usually marinated before cooking, both to flavour and tenderise it: in India meat is cooked until very tender – essential as food is traditionally eaten with the fingers. Try Rogan Josh, regarded as the finest example of the culinary craft of Kashmir – the master chefs of the royal Moghul kitchens boasted about perfecting this dish.

LEFT: *Beef korma;* RIGHT: *Lamb kebabs*

PREETI KABAB
NUGGETS OF LAMB

SERVES 6

1 kg (2 lb) lean lamb, finely minced
1 medium onion, peeled and finely chopped
8 garlic cloves, crushed
4 green chillies, finely chopped
1 tablespoon coriander seeds, ground
2 tablespoons chopped coriander leaves
50 g (2 oz) root ginger, grated
2 teaspoons carom seeds
pinch of bicarbonate of soda
2½ teaspoons salt
2 egg whites, beaten well
6 tablespoons vegetable oil
sauce or chutney to serve

To garnish:
2 onions, peeled and sliced in rings
4 lemons, sliced

Preparation time: 25 minutes
Cooking time: 30 minutes

1. Combine the minced lamb with the onion, garlic, chillies, coriander seeds and leaves, ginger, carom seeds, bicarbonate of soda and salt. Divide the mixture into 18 equal portions and shape them into nuggets.

2. Coat the nuggets in beaten egg white. In a frying pan heat the oil, 1 tablespoon at a time, and fry the nuggets gently in batches until they are all cooked through.

3. Garnish with slices of onion and lemon and serve hot with sauce or chutney of your choice.

PREETI KABAB

This may well be the centrepiece of a dinner party for two, but most Indian meals are meant to be enjoyed by many more people. In a culture where the whole family, including grandparents, cousins and newborn infants, often live together under one roof, and in which innumerable festivals – each calling for a banquet – punctuate the calendar, it is not surprising that Indian dishes lend themselves so well to entertaining. Menu-planning does not apply in the way it is understood in the west, that is, as a sequence of dishes. In India a combination will be devised to be served simultaneously, in a variety which will be as appetizing to look at as it will be delicious to eat. Not only that, in terms of nutritional balance Indian food is extremely healthy, with protein from a number of sources – pulses and eggs as well as meat and fish – matched with a choice of vegetables, some cooked, some freshly pickled, rice and bread, and perhaps a refreshing yogurt raita.

NARGISI KOFTE
NARGISI KOFTA CURRY

SERVES 6

450 g (1 lb) mutton, minced
4 cloves
8 black peppercorns
4 garlic cloves, crushed
1 green chilli, chopped
25 g (1 oz) root ginger, chopped
pinch of salt
150 ml (¼ pint) water
2 tablespoons chick pea flour
1 egg, beaten
6 eggs, hard-boiled
1 egg white, beaten
225 g (8 oz) ghee

Sauce:

50 g (2 oz) ghee
1 large onion, peeled and finely chopped
2 bay leaves
1 × 142 ml (5 fl oz) carton plain
  unsweetened yogurt
salt
2 tablespoons tomato purée
4 tomatoes, peeled and sliced
150 ml (¼ pint) water

Spices:

1 teaspoon turmeric powder
1 teaspoon red chilli powder
1 teaspoon ground coriander
1 teaspoon garam masala

To garnish:

chopped parsley or coriander leaves

Preparation time: 35 minutes
Cooking time: 1 hour
Oven: 180°C, 350°F, Gas Mark 4

LEFT: Nargisi kofta curry

1. Mix the minced meat in a saucepan with the cloves, peppercorns, garlic, green chilli, ginger, salt and water. Simmer, stirring occasionally, for 15 minutes, or until the mixture is dry. Leave until cool.
2. Mix in the chick pea flour and egg and knead until sticky. Divide the mixture into 6 equal portions and flatten them out. Wrap a hard-boiled egg in each one. Brush the beaten egg white over the koftas.
3. Heat the ghee in a frying pan and fry the koftas until they are golden all over. Drain them on absorbent kitchen paper and arrange in a casserole dish.
4. To make the sauce, heat the ghee in a saucepan and fry the onion and bay leaves until they are light brown. Remove the pan from the heat and stir in all the spices. Return to the heat for about 15 seconds, stirring. Add the yogurt and tomato purée and season with salt to taste. Simmer for 5 minutes, stirring continuously. Mix in the tomatoes and water. Bring to the boil, stirring. Pour the sauce over the koftas and cook in a preheated oven for about 15 minutes. Serve hot, garnished with chopped parsley or coriander.

INDIAN FRUIT

Follow a rich dish like Nargisi kofta with a selection of fruit. Although fresh fruit is rarely included on the menus of Indian restaurants, it is an important part of the diet. Choose a large flat platter and include as many exotic varieties as you can. Depending on the season, choose from pineapple, mango, passion fruit, pomegranate, melon, figs, kumquats, lychees, dates, kiwifruit and bananas. Prepare the fruit according to type, peeling, removing seeds where necessary, and cutting into bite-shaped cubes or slices. You can achieve a rainbow effect by arranging the pieces in stripes across the platter or, on a round plate, in wedges of colour like slices of cake. Decorate the platter with orange leaves, sprigs of mint or borage, or flower petals such as marigold, rose or nasturtium, and let your guests eat with their fingers.

YAKHINI KORMA
MUTTON KORMA

750 g (1½ lb) mutton, cut in 2.5 cm (1 inch) cubes
600 ml (1 pint) water
4 cloves
6 black peppercorns
2 × 5 cm (2 inch) pieces cinnamon stick
1 teaspoon black cumin seeds
2 black cardamoms
100 g (4 oz) ghee
2 medium onions, peeled and finely chopped
4 bay leaves
4 garlic cloves, crushed
15 g (½ oz) root ginger, grated
1 teaspoon turmeric powder
1 teaspoon garam masala
1 teaspoon red chilli powder
2 × 142 ml (5 fl oz) cartons plain unsweetened yogurt

To garnish:
1 green chilli, finely chopped
½ teaspoon saffron strands

Preparation time: 20 minutes
Cooking time: 1½ hours

'Mutton' in India is very often goat. Similarly, kid is often described as lamb. This particular dish is cooked in the juices from the meat and is scrumptious and wholesome.

1. Put the mutton in a saucepan with the water. Put the cloves, peppercorns, cinnamon, cumin seeds and cardamoms in a small muslin bag and add it to the pan. Cover and simmer gently until the meat is tender and the water is reduced to half, about 1¼ hours.
2. In another saucepan melt the ghee and add the onion, bay leaves, garlic and ginger. Fry until the onion is golden. Add the turmeric, garam masala and chilli powder and mix well. Cook gently for 5 minutes, stirring continuously. Add the yogurt, season with salt to taste and cook for a further 5 minutes, stirring.
3. Stir in the cooked meat mixture and juices and discard the muslin bag. Simmer over a low heat for 15 minutes.
4. Steep the saffron in 1 tablespoon hot water for 2–3 minutes. Transfer the korma to a heated serving dish and scatter the chopped chilli on top. Sprinkle the saffron over the dish and serve.

RICE

Serve rice, plain or spiced, with a Korma. The best rice is Basmati or 'upland' rice, grown in the foothills of the Himalayas; it has a delicious aroma and nutty taste and a higher nutritional content than other types of rice.

To prepare plain boiled rice for 4, soak 225g (8oz) Basmati rice in water for 30 minutes, then drain the water. Bring 600ml (1 pint) water to the boil, add the rice and ¾ teaspoon salt, half cover the pan and boil for 10 minutes. When the rice is tender, drain of the water, return the pan to the heat, add 2 tablespoons butter and mix thoroughly. Cover and leave over a very low heat for 5 minutes.

RIGHT: Mutton korma

SHAAHI KORMA
BEEF KORMA

2 large onions, peeled and finely chopped
25 g (1 oz) blanched almonds
15 g (½ oz) root ginger, chopped
salt
1 tablespoon roasted coriander seeds
450 g (1 lb) chuck steak, cut into 2.5 cm
  (1 inch) cubes
225 g (8 oz) ghee
4 bay leaves
142 ml (5 fl oz) plain yogurt
150 ml (¼ pint) single cream
½ teaspoon saffron strands
150 ml (¼ pint) water
Korma spice mixture (see page 72)
silver foil, to decorate

Preparation time: 30 minutes, plus
marinating
Cooking time: about 1 hour

As with all other beef recipes, pork or lamb can be substituted for beef. This is a rich and rather sophisticated dish – serve it with pullao rice.

1. Mix together half the onion with the almonds, ginger, salt and coriander seeds, adding the cloves, black cardamom and peppercorns from the spice mixture. Grind them to make a smooth paste. Coat the beef liberally with the prepared paste. Set aside for 2 hours to marinate.
2. Heat the ghee in a saucepan and fry the remaining onion and bay leaves until golden. Take half the fried onion from the pan and set it aside. Add the yogurt, green cardamoms and chilli and turmeric powders to the remaining onion and continue frying until the liquid has dried up. Add the cubes of beef and stir well.
3. Beat the cream with the saffron and add it to the meat mixture with the garam masala and reserved fried onions. Add the water and simmer, covered, for 1 hour, or until the meat is tender. Decorate with a leaf of silver foil, if liked.

MEAT DISHES
Meat dishes based on beef are Muslim in origin, belonging to the central region of India where, in the city of Lucknow, for example, a simple korma would be an everyday meal. A richer variation such as the one given here, which includes almonds, cream and saffron, would be appropriate for a more festive occasion such as a wedding.

SUWAR KA GOSHT AUR PALAK
PORK AND SPINACH

450 g (1 lb) pork, cut up
175 g (6 oz) ghee
1 large onion, peeled and chopped
6 garlic cloves, crushed
4 bay leaves
1 teaspoon white cumin seeds
1 teaspoon turmeric powder
1 teaspoon red chilli powder
225 g (8 oz) tomatoes, peeled and sliced
225 g (8 oz) spinach, chopped
salt
25 g (1 oz) root ginger, grated
1 tablespoon garam masala

Preparation time: 30 minutes
Cooking time: about 2 hours

Spinach adds variety to this popular dish – eat it with bread or rice.

1. Heat the ghee in a saucepan and fry the onion, garlic, bay leaves and cumin seeds until the onion is golden brown.
2. Add the meat to the pan with the turmeric and chilli powders. Stir well and add the tomatoes and spinach. Add salt to taste with the ginger and garam masala. Cover and leave over a low heat for 15 minutes.
3. Remove the lid and continue to cook, stirring, for 5 minutes, until the ghee starts to separate.
4. Add 300 ml (½ pint) water and simmer gently until the pork is tender, about 1½ hours. This dish should be moist, but without too much gravy.

TOP: Beef korma; BOTTOM: Pork and spinach

ROGAN JOSH
MUTTON CURRY

SERVES 6
2 tablespoons ghee
675 g (1½ lb) mutton, cut into 2.5 cm
  (1 inch) cubes
4 bay leaves
2 black cardamoms
6 cloves
6 black peppercorns
1 teaspoon black cumin seeds
2 × 2.5 cm (1 inch) pieces cinnamon stick

Vegetable mixture:
2 tablespoons ghee
1 onion, chopped
4 green cardamoms
4 tablespoons tomato purée
1 × 142 ml (5 fl oz) carton plain
  unsweetened yogurt
1 tablespoon salt
600 ml (1 pint) hot water

Paste:
1 onion, chopped
6 garlic cloves
1 tablespoon coriander seeds, roasted
25 g (1 oz) root ginger, crushed
1 teaspoon red chilli powder
1½ teaspoons turmeric powder

To serve:
1 teaspoon garam masala

Preparation time: 20 minutes
Cooking time: 2½ hours

This is a dish for which authors and connoisseurs have sung paeans of praise. Its making marked the pinnacle of the culinary craft of Kashmir; the master chefs of the royal Moghul kitchens boasted about perfecting the dish. I take pride in presenting it to you.

1. Melt the ghee in a saucepan. Fry the mutton, bay leaves, brown cardamoms, cloves, peppercorns, cumin and cinnamon gently for 15 minutes. Transfer to a plate.
2. For the vegetable mixture, melt the ghee and fry the onion and green cardamoms until golden. Mix in the tomato purée.
3. Grind all the paste ingredients together until quite smooth. Mix the paste into the vegetables and cook, stirring continuously, for 5 minutes. Stir in the mutton, salt and water.
4. Cover and simmer for 2½ hours, or until the meat is tender. Serve sprinkled with the garam masala.

MANGOES
After a substantial meal like Rogan Josh, a piece of tropical fruit makes the ideal dessert. Mangoes are now widely available and make a simple, refreshing conclusion to a spicy meal. The aromatic, orange-coloured flesh is tender, very juicy, and – because of the high natural sugar content – slightly sticky. It is difficult to eat a mango gracefully, but this method is less messy than others. Cut the unpeeled fruit in half lengthways with a sharp knife and remove the stone. With the point of the knife, cut into the flesh criss-cross fashion right through to the peel. Holding the peel, turn the half-fruit inside out so that the cut pieces, still attached to the peel, are exposed like stubby quills and can be bitten off.

RIGHT: Mutton curry

BHARWAAN ANDAY
STUFFED EGGS

1 tablespoon ghee
1 tablespoon chopped onion
2 tablespoons minced beef
salt to taste
1 green chilli, chopped
1 tablespoon shredded fresh coriander
½ teaspoon grated root ginger
1 tablespoon tomato ketchup
4 large eggs, hard-boiled
1 large fresh egg
1 tablespoon cornflour
breadcrumbs, to coat
300 ml (½ pint) vegetable oil
fresh coriander leaves, to garnish

Preparation time: 30 minutes
Cooking time: 30 minutes

1. Heat the ghee in a frying pan until golden. Add the onion, mince, salt, chilli, coriander, ginger and tomato ketchup, and stir-fry for 5 minutes until cooked.
2. Halve the boiled eggs lengthwise. Remove the yolks and add to the mixture. Cook for another 5 minutes and then remove from the heat and cool.
3. Crack the fresh egg into a bowl and stir in the cornflour to make a smooth batter. Place the breadcrumbs on a separate flat dish.
4. Mound the stuffing into the cavities of 4 half eggs and cover with the remaining halves to make complete egg shapes. Dip the eggs into the batter and then roll in the breadcrumbs.
5. Heat the oil in a deep pan to 180°C, 350°F, or until a cube of bread browns in 30 seconds. Deep-fry the eggs one at a time until golden brown. Keep warm.
6. Serve the stuffed eggs hot, garnished with coriander.

PASINDA TIKKA
PORK TIKKA

SERVES 6
750 g (1½ lb) pork, beaten and cut into
  2.5 cm (1 inch) cubes
1 × 142 ml (5 fl oz) carton plain
  unsweetened yogurt
½ tablespoon vinegar
2 teaspoons salt
2 tablespoons ghee

Paste:
4 red chillies
10 garlic cloves, crushed
2 teaspoons garam masala
2 teaspoons grated root ginger

To serve:
2 medium onions, peeled and sliced in rings
6 lemons, sliced
sauce or chutney to taste

Preparation time: 30 minutes plus marinating
Cooking time: 30 minutes

This dish comes from the Punjab. These tikkas taste superlative when barbecued, but even when they are grilled, they taste nothing short of first-class. They can be served as a snack or as a side dish with a main meal. They go down particularly well with drinks.

1. Grind all the paste ingredients together, in a smooth mixture. Place the cubes of pork on a wooden board and prick them with a fork. Mix the yogurt, vinegar, salt and paste together and rub the mixture all over the pork. Leave to marinate for 4 hours.
2. Thread the meat on skewers and cook under a preheated hot grill until tender. Keep turning them over so that they are well cooked on all sides. When the tikkas are cooked, remove them from the skewers and shallow fry them in a little ghee. Serve hot, with the onion rings, slices of lemon and the sauce or chutney of your choosing.

TOP: Stuffed eggs; BOTTOM: Pork tikka

MADHU KABAB
LAMB KEBABS

SERVES 6
675 g (1½ lb) mutton, minced
1 teaspoon grated root ginger
1 large onion, peeled and finely chopped
25 g (1 oz) gram flour
2 green chillies, finely chopped
1 teaspoon green mango powder
1 tablespoon salt
2 tablespoons lemon juice
1 egg
2 tablespoons chopped coriander leaves
50 g (2 oz) ghee, melted

Spices:
½ teaspoon poppy seeds, roasted and
   ground
1 teaspoon garam masala
1 tablespoon yellow or red chilli powder
½ teaspoon freshly ground black pepper
1 teaspoon black cumin seeds, roasted and
   ground
1 tablespoon ground coriander seeds

To garnish:
2 onions, peeled and sliced in rings
4 lemons, quarterd
3 tomatoes, sliced

Preparation time: 1½ hours
Cooking time: 30 minutes

These are the most popular type of kebabs. They can be deep-fried, shallow fried, grilled or roasted on a barbecue. What can be more versatile? They taste good any way, but I prefer to roast them over a barbecue. These kebabs should always be served hot and are good with ketchup. Other meats give just as successful results.

1. Mix the minced meat, ginger, onion, gram flour, chillies, mango powder, salt and lemon juice together with all the spices. Leave for 30 minutes for the flavours to blend. Work in the egg and chopped coriander. Knead this mixture until it becomes sticky.
2. Divide the mixture into 18 portions and form each piece into a sausage shape. Thread the sausages on to skewers – for longer kebabs, flatten the sausages on the skewers.
3. Cook the kebabs under a preheated hot grill or over a charcoal fire, turning them frequently. Brush the kebabs all over with melted ghee as they are cooking. Alternatively, fry the kebabs gently in the melted ghee, turning them frequently. Serve hot, garnished with onion rings, quartered lemons and sliced tomatoes.

KABABS
Kababs are a favourite food in India – equally popular as a snack or a nibble between meals, as they are at mealtimes. Generally speaking, kabab refers to small pieces of meat or minced meat which are grilled or fried, but there are many other versions. Lamb is naturally used a great deal and Seekh kababs (left), made with minced lamb flattened on to skewers, are often found in restaurants. Much less well known are vegetarian versions like Kabab Allahabadi (page 25), a spicy chick pea mixture from Uttar Pradesh in northern India. Machchhi kabab (page 64) is another uncommon version; it is made by forming cooked, flaked white fish into croquettes with a spicy, garlicky onion mixture. Tikka refers to boneless chunks of meat or fish. Served cold, this type of kabab makes excellent finger food for picnics or parties. For a pork version, generally served hot, try Pasinda tikka on page 91.

RIGHT: Lamb kebabs

BREADS

In some parts of India bread is eaten at every meal. They accompany dishes that are dry, roasted, fried or with thick gravies that can be scooped up – there is no rule about which bread accompanies which dish. There is a great deal of variety in these breads. They can be deep-fried, such as Puri or Paratha, or baked on a hot plate or griddle, such as Chapatis. Naan, the flat leavened bread, is traditionally baked in a tandoor oven, but modern ovens make an acceptable substitute.

LEFT TO RIGHT: *Naan, Poppadums, Crumbly deep-fried bread*

DALL KACHORI
PURI STUFFED WITH DHAL

175 g (6 oz) skinless dried black beans
450 g (1 lb) plain flour
1 green chilli, chopped
½ teaspoon salt
vegetable oil for deep frying

Spices:
1 tablespoon aniseeds
1 teaspoon coriander seeds
½ teaspoon white cumin seeds
½ teaspoon red chilli powder
¼ teaspoon asafoetida powder

Preparation time: 15 minutes plus soaking overnight
Cooking time: 20 minutes

1. Soak the beans in water overnight. Rinse in clear water and drain well. Sift the flour into a basin and gradually add enough cold water to make a soft dough. Cover with a damp cloth and leave for 30 minutes.
2. Grind the drained beans with the chilli, salt and all the spices to make the stuffing. Mix well and divide into 16 portions.

3. With wet hands, divide the dough into 16 portions and smear each one with a little of the oil. Flatten them and roll them out into 5 cm (2 inch) diameter rounds.
4. Wrap 1 portion of the stuffing in each round and with greased hands, roll them into smooth balls. Using a rolling pin, flatten each ball into a 7.5 cm (3 inch) round.
5. Heat the oil in a deep frying pan to 180°C, 350°F, or until a cube of bread browns in 30 seconds. Fry the puri one at a time, until golden on both sides.

PHULKE OR TAWE KI ROTI
CHAPATI

SERVES 6
750 g (1½ lb) wholemeal flour
4 tablespoons plain flour
ghee or butter for serving

Preparation time: 45 minutes
Cooking time: 20 minutes

1. Turn the wholemeal flour into a bowl and gradually mix in enough water to make a pliable dough. Leave it to rest for 30 minutes.
2. Knead the dough again then pull off pieces about the size of ping-pong balls. Roll these in the plain flour and flatten them out, using a rolling pin. This should make 12–15 chapatis.
3. Heat a griddle or heavy-bottomed fry-ing pan until it is very hot, then cook each chapati for 15–20 seconds on each side, turning it when brown spots appear underneath. Press lightly all over, using a clean cloth, and the chapati will puff up. Repeat the process with each chapati.
4. Serve the chapatis soon after cooking with plenty of butter as an accompani-ment to any curry, dhal or dry dish. Wrap them in a clean cloth to keep them hot.

KHUSKHUSI PURI
CRUMBLY DEEP FRIED BREAD

450 g (1 lb) plain flour
pinch of salt
75 g (3 oz) ghee or margarine
vegetable oil for deep frying

Preparation time: 25 minutes
Cooking time: 25 minutes

1. Sift the flour and salt into a large basin. Add 50 g (2 oz) of ghee or margarine and rub it in well. Make a well in the centre and gradually add enough water to make a stiff dough. Leave it to rest for 20 minutes.
2. Knead the dough and divide it into 16–18 equal portions. Coat each one with the remaining ghee and flatten them out into 10 cm (4 inch) diameter rounds.

3. Heat the oil in a frying pan to 180°C, 350°F, or until a cube of bread browns in 30 seconds. Deep-fry each round for 10 seconds until golden on both sides. Drain on absorbent kitchen paper and serve on a plate lined with a clean napkin.

CLOCKWISE FROM THE TOP: Puri stuffed with dhal, Chapati, Crumbly deep-fried bread

PARATI PARAUNTHA
LAYERED PARAUNTHA

SERVES 6
750 g (1½ lb) chapati flour
50 g (2 oz) margarine
225 g (8 oz) ghee

Preparation time: 40 minutes
Cooking time: 25 minutes

This is a superior type of parauntha – more filling and tastier than the basic version. They can be eaten with virtually any vegetable or meat dish. Some people eat them for breakfast with yogurt. I'm sure you will like them.

1. Sift the flour into a bowl and rub in the margarine. Gradually add enough warm water to make a smooth, pliable dough. Leave it to rest for 30 minutes.
2. Divide the dough into 18 equal portions. Roll each one into a ball. Flatten them on a floured surface into 10 cm (4 inch) diameter rounds. Spread ¼ teaspoon ghee on the surface of each round and fold them in half, keeping the ghee inside. Repeat the process to achieve a triangular shape. When all the pieces have been rolled and folded, roll them out on a floured surface to 15 cm (6 inches) on each side.
3. Heat a griddle or heavy-bottomed frying pan and spread 1 teaspoon ghee over the surface. Cook each parauntha for 30 seconds on each side, re-greasing the griddle between each turn. Cook the first side again to make sure it is cooked. Dark brown spots should appear on the surface. Serve hot.

NAAN
LEAVENED BAKED BREAD

SERVES 6
350 g (12 oz) plain flour
1½ teaspoons sugar
1 teaspoon salt
½ teaspoon baking powder
15 g (½ oz) fresh yeast
150 ml (¼ pint) warm milk
1 × 142 ml (5 fl oz) carton plain unsweetened yogurt
100 g (4 oz) butter
2 tablespoons poppy seeds

Preparation time: 30 minutes, plus proving
Cooking time: 30 minutes

This great dish comes from the Punjab and goes very well with the tandoori meat dishes as well as vindaloos. Traditionally, naans are baked in clay ovens, but the method given here should suit everybody. They must be eaten fresh and hot, so serve them as you cook them.

1. Sift the flour into a large bowl and stir in the sugar, salt and baking powder. Dissolve the yeast in the milk and stir in the yogurt. Mix thoroughly with the flour to form a dough. Knead the dough until it is smooth. Cover it with a clean cloth and leave it to rise in a warm place for about 4 hours.
2. Divide the risen dough into 12 equal portions and roll them into balls. On a lightly floured surface, flatten the balls into oblong shapes, using both hands and slapping the naan from one hand to another.
3. Lightly grease a griddle or heavy-bottomed frying pan and heat it until it is very hot. Cook the naan on one side only. Spread the raw side with butter and poppy seeds and place under a preheated hot grill. Cook until browned and serve hot.

TOP: Layered parauntha; BOTTOM: Naan

PAPAD
SAVOURY WAFERS OR POPPADUMS

SERVES 6

vegetable oil for frying 12 papads, halved if required

Preparation time: 5 minutes
Cooking time: 5 minutes

Papads are a well-known savoury side dish which add elegance and style to a meal. There are distinct differences between them – the ones sold in the Bengal and Maharashtra are thick and fluffy and rather bland, those in south India are paper thin and very crisp. In Uttar Pradesh and the Delhi regions, they are flavoured with asafoetida and are studded with crushed black pepper and red chilli powder. Papad making is a trade in India and people hand down the skill for generations to obtain perfect results.

1. Two-thirds fill a medium saucepan with oil and heat it to near smoking point. Put a small piece of papad in the pan to see if the temperature of the oil is right. If it sizzles immediately, the oil is ready for frying. Reduce the heat and drop one papad in the pan. Press it down with a ladle to stop it from curling up. It will sizzle and spread out to its full size, about 15 cm (6 inches) in diameter. Turn it over and cook for 3–4 seconds on the other side.

2. Remove the papad from the pan and stand it edgeways on absorbent kitchen paper so that the excess fat is drained off. If not fully crisp, place the papad under a hot grill for a few seconds before serving. Serve fresh and hot, by itself or with vegetarian or non-vegetarian meals.

MOOLI PARAUNTHA
PARAUNTHA STUFFED WITH RADISH

SERVES 6

450 g (1 lb) chapati flour
225 g (8 oz) white radish, grated
100 g (4 oz) onions, peeled and chopped
2 green chillies, finely chopped
½ teaspoon salt
½ teaspoon grated root ginger
225 g (8 oz) ghee

Preparation time: 40 minutes
Cooking time: 20 minutes

A different variety of parauntha which can be eaten on its own if liked – scrumptious and very satisfying. Eat them with potato curry, papad, yogurt or pickles.

1. Sift the flour into a bowl and gradually mix in enough water to form a smooth dough. Cover the bowl with a damp cloth and leave it for 20 minutes.

2. Squeeze the water from the radish and mix the grated flesh with the onions, chillies, salt and ginger, combining them well.

3. Divide the dough into 12 equal pieces. Using a rolling pin on a floured surface, flatten each piece into a 10 cm (4 inch) diameter round. Take 1 tablespoon of the stuffing, place in the middle of a round and enclose it completely, folding in the edges of the dough to make a ball. Roll the ball flat on a floured surface to make a 15 cm (6 inch) round. Repeat the process with the remaining rounds and stuffing.

4. Heat a griddle or heavy-bottomed frying pan until it is very hot. Spread 1 tablespoon of ghee over the surface and place a parauntha on top. Cook it for 15 seconds, and turn it over. Spread 1 teaspoon ghee over the griddle and cook the parauntha for 20 seconds. Turn it over again. Brown spots should appear on both sides when it is cooked. Turn the parauntha as often as necessary until it is cooked. Repeat the process with the remaining paraunthas. Serve each one hot as soon as it is ready.

TOP: Poppadums; BOTTOM: Parauntha stuffed with radish

CHUTNEYS AND PRESERVES

India is the home of chutneys and preserves and no meal is complete without them. Chutneys perk up a meal, giving a contrast of flavour and taste. They boost the appetite generally, and some of them are intended to aid digestion. They go particularly well with bland foods such as dhals and plain boiled rice. Preserves are usually designed to be kept longer, and are often kept for special occasions such as wedding banquets.

LEFT: *Lemon pickle;* RIGHT: *Chilli pickle in lemon juice*

BOONDI RAITA
BATTER DROP RAITA

2 × 142 ml (5 fl oz) cartons plain
  unsweetened yogurt
½ teaspoon black salt
½ teaspoon salt
¼ teaspoon freshly ground black pepper
1½ teaspoons white cumin seeds, roasted
  and ground
100 g (4 oz) boondi (see page 134)
1 teaspoon red chilli powder
1 green chilli, chopped
1 tablespoon chopped mint, coriander leaves
  or parsley

Preparation time: 45 minutes

A truly fantastic side dish! It is my favourite and I'm sure it will be yours too. Serve it with vegetarian or non-vegetarian meals.

1. Beat the yogurt with a fork for 2–3 minutes and add the salts, pepper and half the cumin. Soak the boondi in warm water for 20–30 minutes.
2. Squeeze the water from the boondi using a muslin cloth. Drop the boondi into the yogurt and mix thoroughly. Serve topped with chilli powder, green chilli, chopped herbs of your choice and the remaining cumin.

CHATPATI CHATNI
CHILLIES AND GINGER IN LEMON JUICE

225 g (8 oz) onions, peeled and chopped
50 g (2 oz) root ginger, grated
2 green chillies, coarsely chopped
2 tablespoons chopped coriander leaves
½ teaspoon freshly ground black pepper
1 teaspoon salt
juice of 1 lemon
6 red radishes, sliced finely

Preparation time: 8 minutes
Storage time: 2 days

1. Mix together all the ingredients and serve as a side dish.

AAM CHATNI
MANGO CHUTNEY

100 g (4 oz) green mango, sliced
1 medium green chilli, chopped
1 teaspoon salt
2 tablespoons chopped mint

Preparation time: 10 minutes
Storage time: 3 days

1. Grind all the ingredients together, using a pestle and mortar, to form a thick pulp. Serve as a side dish. For a sweet and sour effect add 1–1½ teaspoons sugar.

CLOCKWISE FROM THE FRONT: Batter drop raita, Chillies and ginger in lemon juice, Mango chutney

KARONDA CHATNI
GOOSEBERRY CHUTNEY

25 g (8 oz) gooseberries, topped and tailed
1½ teaspoons salt
1 medium green chilli, chopped
1 tablespoon chopped mint

Preparation time: 10 minutes
Storage time: 3 days

This accompaniment is a popular way of adding piquancy to a vegetarian meal.

1. Cut the gooseberries in half and remove the seeds. Grind the flesh with all the other ingredients to make a paste. Serve as a side dish.

TAMATAR CHATNI
TOMATO CHUTNEY

2 medium tomatoes, peeled and crushed
4 small spring onions, chopped
1 small green chilli, chopped
1 small piece root ginger, finely chopped
½ teaspoon salt
pinch of freshly ground black pepper
1 teaspoon chopped coriander leaves
1 tablespoon lemon juice

Preparation time: 15 minutes
Storage time: 2 days

Most chutneys are best eaten fresh, and this is no exception. You can, however, store any leftover chutney in the refrigerator for 2 days.

1. Mix all the ingredients together thoroughly. Serve, using a wooden or stainless steel spoon, with any meal.

BAIGAN RAITA
AUBERGINE RAITA

225 g (8 oz) ghee
2 long aubergines, thinly sliced
2 × 142 ml (5 fl oz) cartons plain
  unsweetened yogurt
1 teaspoon salt
1 teaspoon white cumin seeds, roasted and
  ground
1 tablespoon chopped mint
1 green chilli, chopped
½ teaspoon red chilli powder

Preparation time: 15 minutes

A rather unusual dish in the world of raitas. If you like aubergines, you will love it. If preferred, another vegetable suitably prepared, such as marrow or potato, can be substituted.

1. Heat the ghee in a frying pan. Fry the aubergine slices over a moderate heat until they are golden brown and set them aside.
2. Beat the yogurt with the salt, cumin, mint and green chilli. Soak the aubergine slices in the yogurt and serve, sprinkled with the chilli powder.

CLOCKWISE FROM THE TOP: Gooseberry chutney, Tomato chutney, Aubergine raita

SONTH
SWEET SAUCE

100 g (4 oz) seedless tamarind pulp
175 g (6 oz) jaggery (palm sugar)
300 ml (½ pint) warm water
2 teaspoon ghee
1 teaspoon white cumin seeds
½ teaspoon asafoetida powder
50 g (2 oz) dried dates, chopped and
  soaked
25 g (1 oz) sultanas, soaked
1½ teaspoons salt
1 teaspoon red chilli powder
1 teaspoon aniseeds, roasted and ground
1 tablespoon chopped mint leaves or 1
  teaspoon mint sauce

Preparation time: 1 hour, plus soaking
Storage time: 4 days

1. Soak the tamarind and jaggery together in the water for 1½ hours. Mash the mixture thoroughly and press it through a sieve. Discard the tamarind husk. Mix the ginger into a pulp and set aside.
2. Heat the ghee in a frying pan and fry the cumin and asafoetida powder together. Mix in the tamarind pulp and sauté lightly. Add the dates, sultanas, salt and chilli and aniseed powders and mix thoroughly. Bring to the boil, remove the pan from the heat and allow to cool.
3. Add the mint leaves when the mixture is cold. Transfer to a bowl, cover and store in the refrigerator until it is required.

MIRCH KHATTA ACHAAR
CHILLI PICKLE IN LEMON JUICE

10 chillies
large pinch of asafoetida powder
4 teaspoons mustard seeds
1 teaspoon fenugreek seeds
2 teaspoons white cumin seeds
2 teaspoons salt
5 tablespoons lemon juice

Preparation time: 30 minutes, plus pickling

You will like this pickle, even if you are not a great chilli fan. The lemon juice does wonders for it, and it can be made very quickly.

1. Split the chillies down the middle. Roast the asafoetida powder, mustard, fenugreek and cumin seeds and grind them all together.
2. Add the salt to the spices and stuff this mixture into the chillies. Place the chillies in a sterilised glass jar, pour the lemon juice over them and leave the jar outside in the sun or a well-lit, warm place for a day.
3. Shake the jar or bottle in which the pickle is stored before serving.

NOTE: If a warm place is not available, the lemon juice can be heated up a little before it is poured over the chillies.

LEFT: Sweet sauce; RIGHT: Chilli pickle in lemon juice

NEEBU SIRKA ACHAAR
LEMON PICKLE IN VINEGAR

35 lemons
1.2 litres (2 pints) water
1 teaspoon asafoetida powder
4 teaspoons salt
30 black peppercorns
2 teaspoons brown cardamom seeds
2 tablespoons salt
2 teaspoons red chilli powder
1 tablespoon white cumin seeds
15 cloves
2 tablespoons sugar
2 tablespoons vinegar

Preparation time: 30 minutes
Pickling time: 10 to 15 days
Storage time: 2 months

1. Wash and clean the lemons. Boil the water in a large pan and put 35 lemons in it for 2–3 minutes. Take them out, dry them and cut into quarters.
2. Using sterilised jars for the pickle, sprinkle the asafoetida powder and half the salt over the base. Grind the remaining ingredients together to make a smooth mixture and smear it all over the lemon quarters. Drop these spiced lemon pieces into the jars. Squeeze the juice from the remaining lemons over them and sprinkle with the rest of the salt.
3. Cover the jars with clean cloths and leave out in the sun or in a well-lit and warm place. The pickle should be ready in about 2 weeks.

SEB KA MURABBA
APPLE PRESERVE

750 g (1½ lb) medium cooking apples
2 teaspoons edible lime powder
1.2 litres (2 pints) water
1 kg (2 lb) sugar
600 ml (1 pint) water
2 tablespoons rose water

Preparation time: 15 minutes, plus soaking
Cooking time: 25 minutes
Storage time: 5 days

1. Wash the apples and slice the tops and bottoms off, then prick the whole apples all over, using a fork. Mix the edible lime and water and soak the apples in this mixture for 30 minutes. Rinse the apples in cold running water several times and dry them completely with a clean cloth.
2. Make a syrup by dissolving the sugar in the water over a low heat. Boil the syrup gently until it reaches the thread stage (107°/225°F) and add the apples. Continue boiling until the apples are completely cooked. Remove from the pan and allow to cool.
3. Serve each apple with a little syrup and rose water.

GAJAR KA MURABBA
CARROT PRESERVE

1 kg (2 lb) carrots, peeled and cored
1 kg (2 lb) sugar
600 ml (1 pint) water
juice of 1 lemon
½ teaspoon cardamom seeds, crushed

FROM THE TOP: Lemon pickle in vinegar, Apple preserve, Carrot preserve

Preparation time: 45 minutes
Cooking time: 25 minutes
Storage time: 1 week

1. Cut the carrots into large pieces and prick them all over with a fork. Put the pieces in a saucepan with enough water to cover and bring to the boil. As soon as the water has boiled, remove from the heat and drain off all the water.
2. Dissolve the sugar in the water and boil gently until it reaches the soft ball stage (118°C/245°F). Add the carrot to the syrup and stir in the lemon juice. Continue cooking over a low heat until the carrot is tender and the syrup is thick. Allow to cool completely before stirring in the ground cardamom.

PUDDINGS AND DESSERTS

Few Indian restaurants offer much in the way of desserts, so most Westerners are unaware of the variety of puddings, desserts and sweet-meats served throughout India. Many contain sugar and milk, such as Kulfi, the classic Indian ice cream, and their consistency is much like creamy pudding or foamy custard.

LEFT TO RIGHT: *Batter coils, Coconut toffee, Banana and satsuma pudding*

BESAN LADDU
CHICK PEA NUT BALLS

SERVES 6
225 g (8 oz) ghee
225 g (8 oz) chick pea flour
350 g (12 oz) caster sugar
1 teaspoon chopped cashew nuts
1 teaspoon chopped almonds
1 teaspoon chopped pistachios

Preparation time: 5 minutes
Cooking time: 20 minutes

Laddus are great balls of nourishing fun, to eat before, during or after meals. There are many varieties of this dish, but besan laddus are my particular favourites. They may be served hot or cold.

1. Place the ghee and chick pea flour in a pan over a low heat. Keep stirring to avoid the formation of lumps. When it is cooked, it will release an appetising and aromatic smell. Remove the pan from the heat and let it cool.
2. Add the sugar and nuts to the chick pea mixture and stir them thoroughly. Mould the mixture into small balls of the required size.

NARIYAL BURFI
COCONUT TOFFEE

SERVES 6
225 g (8 oz) coconut, fresh or dry, ground
225 g (8 oz) khoya (see page 134)
1 tablespoon ghee
1 teaspoon cardamom seeds, coarsely ground
500 g (1¼ lb) sugar
450 ml (¾ pint) water
½ tablespoon grated pistachios
½ tablespoon grated almonds

Preparation time: 40 minutes
Cooking time: 15 minutes

1. Mix the coconut and khoya together. Fry them lightly in the ghee over a low heat. Add the cardamom and mix thoroughly.
2. Dissolve the sugar in the water over a low heat and boil gently until it reaches the soft ball stage (118°C/245°F). Stir the coconut mixture into the syrup.
3. Grease a large flat plate and sprinkle the grated nuts over it. Spread the khoya mixture over the plate and let it cool. Using a sharp knife, cut the cooled toffee into squares or diamonds. Turn them over so that the nut-covered side is on the top and serve cold.

JAIPUR PAAG
GRAM FLOUR DIAMONDS

SERVES 6
3 tablespoons water
175 g (6 oz) sugar
100 g (4 oz) gram flour
225 g (8 oz) ghee

To decorate:
1 teaspoon flaked almonds
1 teaspoon chopped pistachios

Preparation time: 5 minutes
Cooking time: 30 minutes

This is a sweetmeat for all seasons, but do not let young children eat too many of them as they are very sweet.

1. Place the water in a large pan over a moderate heat and dissolve the sugar in it. Add the gram flour and stir well to dissolve any lumps.
2. Heat the ghee in a separate pan and keep it on one side.
3. When the gram flour mixture begins to bubble, add the hot ghee a little at a time. Stir continuously, keeping the heat at moderate. The mixture will thicken as it cooks. Eventually it will become bubbly, like a honeycomb. At this point remove the pan from the heat.
4. Spread the mixture evenly on a greased flat plate and cut it into diamond shapes while still warm. Sprinkle the nuts on the top and serve warm or cold.

LEFT TO RIGHT: Chick pea nut balls, Coconut toffee, Gram flour diamonds

SUJI HALWA
SEMOLINA SWEET

SERVES 6
175 g (6 oz) ghee
175 g (6 oz) fine semolina
150 ml (¼ pint) water
50 g (2 oz) seedless raisins, soaked
25 g (1 oz) desiccated coconut (optional)
25 g (1 oz) almonds, shredded
1 teaspoon green cardamom seeds, ground
100 g (4 oz) sugar

Preparation time: 10 minutes
Cooking time: 20 minutes

This dish is a standard offering at all the Sikh religious gatherings. It is a light food for the breakfast table and is universally popular.

1. Melt the ghee over a low heat in a frying pan. Add the semolina and fry for about 10 minutes, stirring continuously. Now add the water, raisins, coconut (if used) and half each of the almonds and ground cardamom seeds. When the water is fully absorbed, add the sugar. Keep stirring until the ingredients are well mixed.
2. Remove the pan from the heat and pour the mixture into 6 individual bowls. Sprinkle the semolina with the remaining almonds and the cardamom and serve hot.

SHANTI SANDESH
MESSAGE OF PEACE DISCS

150 g (5 oz) sugar
225 (8 oz) paneer (see page 138)
1 tablespoon rose water
½ teaspoon green cardamom seeds, coarsely ground
10 pistachios, thinly sliced and crushed

Preparation time: 10 minutes
Cooking time: 30 minutes

This sweetmeat is especially liked by students and those engaged in intellectual work. They sell by the billion in India during the examination period.

1. In a bowl, mix together the sugar and the paneer. Transfer the mixture to a small saucepan placed over a low heat. Stir it quickly and continuously in order to avoid the formation of lumps. When the mixture solidifies, splash the rose water on it and remove the pan from the heat. Stir a few more times.
2. Spread the pistachio and cardamom crumbs on 2 separate plates. Divide the mixture into 8 or 12 balls and flatten them to give disc shapes. Press 1 side of each disc into both plates in turn so that the front of the sandesh is coated with crumbs. Serve cold.

MOHIT SHARBAT
LEMON SHERBET

juice of 1 lemon
175 g (6 oz) sugar
600 ml (1 pint) water
4 drops kewra essence
8 ice cubes, crushed

To decorate:
4 lemon slices

Preparation time: 50 minutes

This sherbet is one of the most popular; athletes are particularly partial to it because no other drink is as refreshing after strenuous activity.

1. Mix the lemon juice, sugar and 1 cup of the water in the electric blender. Add the remaining water and the kewra essence and blend again for a few seconds more.
2. Place 1 tablespoon of the sherbet in each of 4 individual ice cube containers and freeze.
3. Refrigerate the remaining sherbet for 30 minutes. To serve, stir and pour into 4 glasses. Add crushed ice and 1 lemon ice cube to each glass and decorate with a slice of lemon.

LEFT TO RIGHT: Semolina sweet, Message of peace discs, Lemon sherbet

JALEBI
BATTER COILS IN SYRUP

175 g (6 oz) plain flour
50 g (2 oz) gram flour, lightly fried
4 tablespoons plain unsweetened yogurt
10 g (¼ oz) fresh yeast
300 ml (½ pint) water
225 g (8 oz) sugar
½ teaspoon saffron powder
½ teaspoon green cardamom seeds, ground
vegetable oil for deep frying

Preparation time: 15 minutes, plus proving
Cooking time: 20 minutes

Jalebis are the youngsters' finger-licking favourites. They are easy to make and are very refreshing first thing in the mornings. The secret of this sweet is that they should be eaten soon after being made, when they are crisp and hot, otherwise they become soft and unappetising.

1. In a large bowl, mix the flours with the yogurt, yeast and water to form a thick creamy batter. Set aside for about 2 hours to ferment.
2. Place the water and sugar in a saucepan over a low heat and stir until the sugar has dissolved. Bring to the boil, stirring, and cook until the syrup has reached the thread stage (107°C/225°F on a sugar thermometer). Just before the syrup is ready, add the saffron powder and ground cardamom.
3. Heat the oil until a cube of day-old bread turns golden in 1 minute. Whisk the batter thoroughly. Pour the batter in a steady stream through a baster (or coconut shell with a hole) into the pan to form coils. Make a few at a time. Deep-fry the coils for about 30 seconds. Turn them to ensure that they are golden and crisp but not brown all over.
4. Remove the coils from the pan and drain them on absorbent kitchen paper. Immerse them in the prepared syrup for 3–4 minutes so that they can soak up as much syrup as possible. Take them out of the syrup, and serve hot.

NAARIYAL KHEER
COCONUT PUDDING

75 g (3 oz) sugar
900 ml (1½ pints) creamy milk
50 g (2 oz) ghee
100 g (4 oz) coconut, fresh or dry, grated
1 teaspoon green cardamom seeds
25 g (1 oz) sultanas
25 g (1 oz) flaked almonds
25 g (1 oz) pistachios, chopped
15 g (½ oz) whole chironju (sweet almonds)

To decorate:
½ teaspoon saffron strands
2 tablespoons rose water

Preparation time: 5 minutes
Cooking time: 45 minutes

I am sure this superb pudding will be a hit with all in your family after its very first appearance. The coconut, the dry fruits and the rose water all lend this dish a distinctive Indian flavour.

1. Pour the sugar and milk into a saucepan and bring them to the boil gradually. Once it comes to the boil, remove from the heat for a minute. Return to the heat and again bring to the boil. Remove the pan from the heat after the second boiling and put it to one side.
2. Heat the ghee in a clean pan and gently fry the grated coconut until it is golden. Add the warm sweetened milk and cook over a low heat, stirring continuously as it thickens.
3. When the milk is reduced by half, add the cardamom, sultanas and nuts and continue to cook for 5 minutes, still stirring.
4. Pour the mixture into a serving bowl and leave it to cool. Before serving, sprinkle the pudding with the saffron and rose water.

Top: Batter coils in syrup; BOTTOM: Coconut pudding

GULAAB JAAMUN
CREAM CHEESE BALLS IN SYRUP

SERVES 6
225 g (8 oz) khoya
25 g (1 oz) flour
40 g (1½ oz) paneer (see page 138)
12 small pieces sugar candy
300 ml (½ pint) water
225 g (8 oz) ghee

To Serve:
2 tablespoons rose water

Preparation time: 30 minutes
Cooking time: 30 minutes

This universally liked dish is soft and syrupy and tastes gorgeous!

1. Mix the khoya, flour and paneer together and form the mixture into 12 small balls. Wrap a piece of sugar candy in each piece of the mixture.
2. Dissolve the sugar in the water. Boil the syrup gently to the thread stage (107°C/225°F). To test, drop a little syrup from a spoon on to a dish. The syrup should form a fine, thin thread.
3. Heat the ghee in a saucepan to 180°C, 350°F or until a cube of bread browns in 30 seconds. Fry the balls until golden all over.
4. Drain the balls on absorbent kitchen paper then immerse them in the syrup. Leave for about 10 minutes before eating. Sprinkle with rose water before serving.

KELA, SANTARA KHEER
BANANA AND SATSUMA PUDDING

2 teaspoons sugar
½ teaspoon freshly ground black pepper
½ teaspoon red chilli powder
1 teaspoon salt
2 × 142 ml (5 fl oz) cartons plain unsweetened yogurt
2 large bananas, peeled and thinly sliced
2 large satsumas, peeled, segmented, pith and pips removed
½ teaspoon saffron strands

Preparation time: 20 minutes

1. In a bowl, mix together the sugar, pepper, chilli powder, salt and yogurt. Add the bananas and satsumas and mix together for about 2 minutes.
2. Steep the saffron in a teaspoon of warm water and sprinkle it over the dish before serving.

TOP: Cream cheese balls in syrup; BOTTOM: Banana and satsuma pudding

MEETHA SHARBAT
YOGURT SHERBET

SERVES 6
600 ml (1 pint) plain unsweetened yogurt
4 tablespoons sugar
1 tablespoon vanilla or other chosen essence
900 ml (1½ pints) ice-cold water
12 ice cubes, crushed

To decorate:
25 g (1 oz) flaked almonds

Preparation time: 5 minutes

This is a high-speed cold drink. No sooner have you thought about it, you can be sipping it.

1. Mix the yogurt, sugar, essence and water together and mix in the electric blender. Process on high speed for about 1 minute.
2. Pour the frothy yogurt liquid into 6 individual glasses. Add the crushed ice and sprinkle the flaked almonds on top of each glass before serving.

KUNWAR KULFI
KULFI FOR THE PRINCES

900 ml (1½ pints) creamy milk
225 g (8 oz) khoya (see page 134) or
  condensed milk
225 g (8 oz) sugar
50 g (2 oz) flaked almonds
25 g (1 oz) pistachios, chopped
175 g (6 oz) peaches, pears and pineapple,
  fresh or canned, drained and diced
1 teaspoon green cardamom powder
4 drops of kewra essence or 2 tablespoons
  rose water

To decorate:
25 g (1 oz) pistachios, grated

Preparation time: 45 minutes plus freezing
Cooking time: 2 hours

Use whatever selection of fruit you prefer, according to what is available. Fruit essence in sufficient quantities can also be used to replace part or all of the fruit.

1. Boil the milk and leave it to simmer over a low heat for about 20 minutes. Keep stirring, taking care that the milk does not boil over. Still keeping the pan on the heat, add the khoya or condensed milk. If using khoya, add it gradually; if using condensed milk, add it in one go. Add the sugar, almonds and pistachios, mix well and cook for a further 15 minutes, stirring occasionally.
2. Remove the pan from the heat and let it cool a little. Add the fruit, cardamom powder and kewra essence or rose water. Mix well with a spoon, taking care not to mash the fruit, and pour into 4 individual moulds.
3. Place the moulds in the freezer for about 1 hour until the kulfi is solid. Transfer to the refrigerator at this stage if it is to be served later. Serve straight from the refrigerator, as the kulfi will melt quickly if left outside. Decorate each serving with grated pistachios.

CLOKWISE FROM THE FRONT: Kulfi for the princes, Yogurt sherbet, Blackberry sherbet (page 124), Whitegourd sweetmeat (page 124)

PHAALSA PAWAN BASERA
BLACKBERRY SHERBET

SERVES 6
450 g (1 lb) blackberries
900 ml (1½ pints) water
450 g (1 lb) caster sugar
12 ice cubes, crushed

To decorate:
6 pineapple rings

Preparation time: 1½ hours, plus soaking

1. Lightly crush the blackberries in a basin and add the water. Leave to soak for 6–8 hours. During this soaking time the water will draw all the colour from the blackberries.
2. Mash the blackberries thoroughly with the water. Strain the mixture through a muslin cloth, or press through a fine sieve into a bowl. Add the sugar and stir well until it has dissolved.
3. Place 1 tablespoon of the sherbet in each of 6 individual ice cube containers and freeze.
4. Refrigerate the sherbet for at least 1 hour. Pour into 6 tall glasses, add some crushed ice and place 1 sherbet ice cube in each glass. Serve decorated with pineapple rings.

PETHA
WHITEGOURD SWEETMEAT

SERVES 6
450 g (1lb) whitegourd flesh, cut into cubes
1 teaspoon edible lime powder
450 ml (¾ pint) water
575 g (1¼ lb) sugar

To garnish:
6 pieces silver foil (see page 135)

To serve:
2 tablespoons rose water

Preparation time: 5 minutes, plus soaking time
Cooking time: 35 minutes

This dish is a famous offering from Agra, the city renowned for the Taj Mahal. Eat it with syrup or dry – for the latter version, continue cooking until the sugar granulates.

1. Prick the whitegourd cubes all over with a fork. Mix the edible lime powder with sufficient water to cover all the cubes in a large pan. Leave overnight or for 8 hours. Drain the cubes and rinse several times in cold running water.
2. Dissolve the sugar in the water over a low heat. Boil gently to 107°C/225°F. To test, drop a little syrup from a spoon on to a dish. The syrup should form a fine, thin thread. Lower the drained cubes into the boiling syrup and cook over a moderate heat for about 20 minutes. Check the syrup from time to time to see that it is not getting too thick.
3. When the syrup has completely soaked into the cubes, remove the pan from the heat and leave to cool.
4. Cover the cubes with the foil and serve with the rose water sprinkled on top.

$\mathcal{F}$OOD FACTS

HELEN DORE

INDIAN COOKING

The vast, teeming sub-continent of India offers a cuisine full of subtlety and variety – far more so than most menus in Indian restaurants in the West might suggest. This is largely because the population of India consists of a multiplicity of races and creeds, all with their own special dietary laws. For example, the Hindus and Sikhs do not eat beef, the cow being sacred in Indian mythology; indeed India has long been the undisputed world centre of vegetarianism, with some 400 million Hindus strict vegetarians.

The extended family is a feature of Indian society at all levels, and the fact that in many households a number of generations will be found living under the same roof is one of the reasons why Indian cooking remains strongly traditional. Recipes are passed from mother to daughter, aunt to niece, grandmother to grand-daughter, each with its own individual flavour and personal touch. In fact it is said that Indian cooks have 'taste in their hands', and that every recipe is given a different interpretation by individual cooks.

Festivals

In India large family gatherings are everyday events to a much greater extent than in the West, and food does of course feature prominently at these. The Indian calendar also contains literally hundreds of festivals, with special dishes for all of them, and to offer food is one of the most important expressions of the warmth and hospitality for which the Indians are renowned. Thus from many points of view food plays a tremendously important part in the Indian way of life.

For most people, the spiciness of Indian food is its most outstanding characteristic. The use of spices is indeed one of the great arts of Indian cookery, but contrary to popular belief this does not necessarily mean that spiced dishes are always hot. Rather, it is the combination of individual spices that gives Indian food its highly aromatic character – Indian dishes are not dominated by the flavour of a single spice, but by special subtle mixtures, some of which can be found on pages 132-33. There is more information about spices, too, on pages 130-31.

India being such a huge country, it is not surprising that the cuisine varies considerably from one region to another. Each region boasts its own traditional specialities, its preferred breads and grains, its own bias towards meat, fish or vegetables, depending on religious preference as well as geography.

REGIONAL COOKING

The East
In the east, Bihar and Bengal, with the estuary of the mighty river Ganges, have an abundance of fish and seafood, cooked in a great variety of ways. No meal is complete for a Bengali without fish in one form or another. Mustard seeds and mustard oil are both widely used in the cooking of this region.

The North
The north boasts Moghul cuisine, the most sophisticated of the regional styles of cooking. Kashmir is noted for the perfection of its curries, subtly flavoured with warm, mellow spices like cinnamon, cardamom, mace, nutmeg, cloves and saffron, especially its mild, creamy *kormas*. Also in the north, the Punjab is the home of tandoori cooking, the famous method by which food marinated in a spicy paste is cooked over charcoal in special clay ovens (*tandoor*). The sides of the *tandoor*, lined with special smooth clay, are used for baking bread: the Punjab is an important wheat-growing area. Rice is also a staple crop, and it is here in the far north that the superb Basmati rice is grown.

The South
In contrast with the north, South Indian curries are thin and fiery; this is specially true of vindaloo dishes. In fact, in South India even mild curries are hotter than hot curries elsewhere! South India is also a stronghold of the Hindus, with vegetable dishes and rice as their staple foods. Fresh vegetables, particularly potatoes, beans, peas, spinach, cauliflowers, okra and aubergines, are put to delicious use in all kinds of

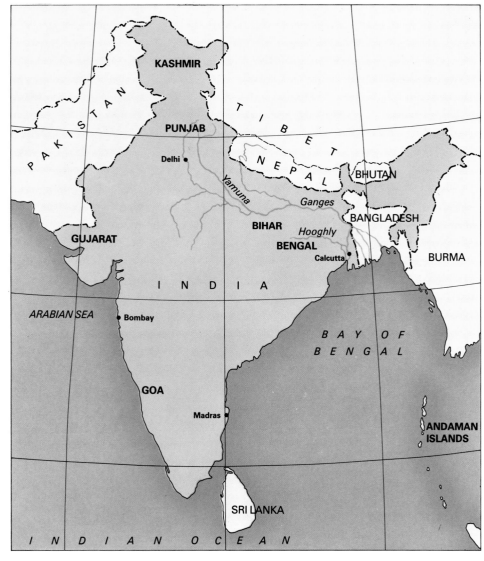

India is similar to Europe in that each state has its own language, culture and foods, as well as its own dominant religions. Some have traditions that go back 1,000 years. Major influences in the past were the Muslim rule, which began in the 11th century, and later, British colonization.

dishes, and there is a great variety of pulses, which feature widely on many vegetarian menus, often in puréed form, as a side dish: pigeon and chick peas, mung and black beans and lentils are especially popular.

The West
Gujarat has a highly distinctive vegetarian cuisine, flavoured with red chillies pounded with garlic, cumin and coriander. Much of the food is based on grains, especially millet, as well as beans, roots and vegetables. Parsi food, on the

other hand, combines the Gujarati love of sweet and sour flavours with Persian-style mixtures of meat and dried fruit. Further south, Bombay's markets display a wealth of fruit and fish – including the deliciously flavoured pomfret – while its street vendors sell spicy snacks.

STAPLE FOODS

Rice dishes range from the very simple to the very sophisticated: the rice may be plain-boiled as an accompaniment; mixed with a pulse, especially black beans; or combined with other ingredients to make elegant pilaus and biryanis. The traditional festive dish served at a Moslem wedding is a pilau of

rice, orange peel, sultanas and nuts. Basmati rice, with its slender grains and distinctive nutty flavour, from the foothills of the Himalayas, is the finest type of rice.

Breads

A variety of unique breads (*roti*) make an important contribution to the Indian vegetarian diet, and indeed to any Indian meal. They are all quite different: *naan* is traditionally baked in the tandoor oven and may be served plain or with a delicious stuffing mixture. *Chapattis* are cooked over a griddle, rather like pancakes. *Puri,* small round discs of dough, are deep-fried, and are usually served for special occasions. *Parauntha* are triangular and shallow-fried.

Chutneys and pickles, made with vegetables, fruits and herbs, with lots of pungent garlic, ginger and chilli, are essential to the enjoyment of an Indian meal. Indian chutneys are usually uncooked – the ingredients are simply chopped or pounded to a paste – and are of thinner consistency than Western chutneys.

Yogurt-based *raitas,* served as side dishes, rather like a cross between a sauce and a salad, also make refreshing accompaniments to Indian food. In fact yogurt is also an indispensable ingredient in cooking, as a thickening agent in sauces, and as a tenderizing agent in marinades for kebabs and *tikkas.* In Indian households yogurt is made freshly every day from buffalo rather than cow's milk, which gives it its thick, creamy texture.

Sweetmeats Indians have very sweet teeth, and desserts and sweetmeats are very popular: they are traditionally offered to guests as a sign of welcome. Many Indian sweets are milk-based and are very rich and sustaining. Semolina and rice are often used in Indian desserts, but with very different results from milk puddings as we know them in the West. The milk has to be specially boiled down, and a recipe for this is given on page 134, along with some of the other special preparations unique to Indian cuisine: these include the basic sugar syrup which features widely in Indian sweet-making. For special

SERVING AN INDIAN MEAL

Basically, Indian food falls into five main categories: appetizers, main dishes, side dishes, accompanying staples – rice and bread and pulses – and sweets. Starters and puddings as we know them in the West are not traditionally part of an Indian meal, in which all the dishes are served together rather than in separate courses. Along with the main dishes, whether vegetarian or containing meat, poultry, fish, seafood and eggs, a selection of side dishes is served: vegetable preparations, dhal, poppadums, chutney, raitas and so on. Rice and/or bread is always served with an Indian meal. The various dishes are often served in small bowls set in *thali,* large rimmed metal plates. Indians like

to eat with their fingers, which they believe is the best way of relishing the flavour of the food, using one of the pliable Indian breads as a scoop.

Drinks

In India iced water and fresh fruit and yogurt drinks (see Almond Lassi recipe) would be served rather than wine. However, chilled rosé and dry white wine would go well with Indian fish and seafood dishes, and robust red wine with heartier meat dishes. Cold beer is always very acceptable too with Indian food. Fragrant spiced teas are also very popular, particularly after a meal, when they provide a suitable finish to elaborately spiced dishes. These teas are fragrant with cinnamon, cardamom,

cloves and even essences such as rose and sandalwood.

At the conclusion of a dinner in India, *paans* are served. The *paan* is a heart-shaped leaf spread with lime paste and stuffed with chopped betel nuts, then folded into a triangle. It is secured with a clove and served wrapped in a damp cloth in a special *paan* dish. The Indians chew *paans* rather as one might smoke a cigar.

Sweetmeats

If you have concluded the meal with fresh fruit, always very welcome after spicy food, you might like to serve a dish of sweetmeats with coffee or tea. Try decorating the sweets as the Indians do, with silver foil or *vark,* which is silver occasions, sweets are traditionally decorated with wafer-thin gold or silver edible foil, which gives a spectacular finish to a dish piled high with sweetmeats. Indian ice creams, called *kulfi,* are especially delicious.

Snacks Throughout India savoury snacks are tremendously popular, for a light lunch, picnics, with drinks, or just to nibble throughout the day. They are sold by street vendors and are also available at special *chaat* shops (see page 11) which usually open in the early evening. These snacks include onion *bhaaji* (onion rings dipped in batter and deep-fried); vegetarian and non-vegetarian samosas, deep-fried triangular pasties; kebabs; chicken drumsticks; courgettes; aubergine fritters; spiced or plain poppadums and many other savoury titbits. These would be washed down with *lassi,* a deliciously tangy yogurt-based drink, or a refreshing fresh fruit *sharbat,* or with one of the many interesting varieties of tea.

dust compressed into wafer-thin foil. Silver foil is sold between two sheets of paper: to apply it, carefully peel off the top sheet of paper, then lift the silver foil, with the bottom sheet of paper still attached, and invert it over the dish. Gently peel away the paper.

EQUIPMENT

If you are going to cook authentic Indian food, do you need any special equipment?

For those of you who already have a well-equipped kitchen, the answer is probably 'no'. Good knives, sturdy pans with a good distribution of heat, rolling pins, graters, bowls, slotted spoons, pestle and mortar, and frying pans are to be found in most kitchens.

There are, however, a few items that make the cooking of Indian food simpler.

Food processor or blender
Every Indian home has a grinding stone. This consists of a large, flat stone that just sits and a smaller one that is moved manually on top of it and does the actual grinding. Their place, in modern kitchens, can be taken by good processors and blenders. Onions, garlic and ginger, formerly ground on grinding stones, can now be made into a paste in machines.

If you do not have a food processor or blender, then there are ways around this. Garlic, for example, may be mashed in a mortar or put through a garlic press. Ginger may be grated on the finest part of the grater. Onions can just be chopped very finely.

Electric coffee grinder
Food processors and blenders cannot do all the work of an Indian grinding stone. Dry spices, for example, cannot be ground in them properly. For this, only a coffee-grinder will do. A coffee-grinder grinds spices in seconds and can then be wiped clean. If you do not have one, you will have to crush your spices in small quantities with a pestle and mortar.

Large non-stick frying pan with a lid
Non-stick pans take the worry out of cooking many foods. Browning meats do not stick to the bottom, nor do sauces with ginger or almonds. As metal spoons ruin the finish of non-stick utensils, use plastic or wooden ones.

Cast-iron frying pans
A cast-iron frying pan is needed for roasting spices – it can heat without oil or water in it. A larger cast-iron pan is excellent for making Indian breads such as *parathas* and *chapatis.* In India, these breads are cooked on a *tava,* a round, concave cast-iron plate. A large cast-iron frying pan makes the best substitute.

Electric rice cooker
If you frequently cook large quantities of rice, an electric rice cooker can be a useful piece of equipment. The cooker has a large covered pan which sits on top of an electric element. When the water has been absorbed by the rice, the cooker switches itself off, and will then keep the rice warm for several hours. The preparation of the rice and the amount of water you use to cook it in are identical to the conventional methods of cooking rice.

Woks
The Indian wok (*Kadhai*) looks like a round-bottomed casserole, and is very useful for deep-frying and stir-frying vegetables. You can of course use a frying pan for stir-frying, but if you already possess a Chinese wok, this would work equally well.

SPICES IN INDIAN CUISINE

In Indian cooking spices are used not only to lend a dish fragrance or piquancy, but also to give colour and hotness. They may also serve to thicken sauces, or to tenderize meat and poultry. The latter use is particularly valuable, as in India meat is not hung as it is in the West, because of the hot climate, and so can be tough.

Spices have medicinal properties, too.

Indians often chew a few spices after a meal, to help digestion, rather as after-dinner mints are served with coffee in the West. The classic spices for this purpose are fennel seeds, cardamom and cloves. Spices also encourage perspiration, essential for keeping cool and fresh in a hot climate, and this is why Indians prefer spicy food – which to a Westerner might not also perhaps seem ideal fare at high temperatures.

For some of the classic Indian spice mixtures see pages 132-133.

It is best to buy spices whole, to be freshly ground as required, for maximum aroma. Store spices in airtight containers in a cool, dry place, to prevent them from becoming rancid.

SPICE CHART

Asafoetida: A huge member of the parsley family. The evil-smelling sap from the plant's stem and roots solidifies into a brown lump which gives a pungent, buff-coloured powder. When used in minute quantities it is a remarkable enhancer of other flavours. The frightful smell disappears in cooking.

Cardamom: The pods are either small and green or large and black, with small, aromatic black seeds. The whole seed-pod is used more often than the individual seeds. Green cardamom is widely used in sweets and desserts. 'Black' cardamom (which is actually brown) is used in savoury dishes and is one of the main spices in Garam Masala (see page 132). The aroma of cardamom is unique and unmistakable; its flavour is sweet, with a hint of eucalyptus. Buy the pods whole and store them in an airtight container.

Carom seeds: A digestive spice used as a seasoning.

Chilli comes in a wide variety of strengths, from mild to very hot. Red chillies are sold dried, either whole or in powder form. For the flavour without the heat, remove the seeds from whole chillies.

Cinnamon: A warm spice, another of the Garam Masala spices. The dried bark of an evergreen, the long sticks or quills are

sometimes used as a garnish for Indian dishes, as well as being ground for use in cooking. The power is convenient to buy, but the sticks of cinnamon keep their flavour longer.

Cloves: Widely used to flavour savoury dishes, in either whole or ground form.

Cloves are unopened flower buds which dry to a deep rich brown and resemble small tacks in shape. They are both sweet and pungent. It is best to buy them whole, and grind as necessary.

Coriander seeds: One of the essential Garam Masala spices, and also used to thicken sauces and gravies as well as to flavour food. They have a delicious nutty aroma. Ground roasted coriander seed is often used as a garnish for yogurt dips and salads.

Cumin seed: Cumin seeds come from a plant of the parsley family. The small, boat-shaped seeds have a strong, unmistakable aroma, sweetish and warming. The flavour is penetrating, and cumin should be used in moderation. It is one of the most commonly used spices in India, both to cook with and to sprinkle over *chaat* or *raita*, as a garnish.

Curry leaves: Small shiny evergreen leaves, rather like small bay leaves. These aromatic leaves are usually chopped and fried, at the start of making curry. Like bay leaves, they can be used fresh or dried. The dried leaves may also be ground to a powder.

Fennel seeds have a sweetish, liquorice taste and are sometimes used in sweet as well as savoury dishes.

USING SPICES

Grinding and Crushing Spices

Spices are best ground or crushed in small quantities in a mortar with a pestle. For grinding larger quantities an electric coffee grinder, kept specially for spices, is very useful.

When spices need to be crushed rather than ground to a fine powder, place them in a polythene bag and crush them with a rolling pin.

Dry-Roasting Spices

A heavy frying pan, ideally made of cast iron, is also ideal for this purpose. Add the spices and roast, stirring and shaking the pan constantly to prevent them from catching and burning. After a couple of minutes they will begin to colour and release their aroma. Continue stirring and shaking until the spices are dark brown, watching them very carefully all the time.

Frying Spices

In Indian cookery spices are often used to flavour fat for frying. Heat some *ghee* or oil in a heavy frying pan and when it is really hot – sizzling but not smoking – add the spices, which will turn brown almost immediately. Take great care not to let them burn. The temperature of the fat or oil is crucial to this process, and as with so many Indian cookery techniques, practice will help you get it just right.

Fenugreek: The pods of the fenugreek plant contain tiny, pebble-like seeds. Only when roasted do the seeds give off their pungent aroma. The taste is bitter-sweet and powerful. Widely used in vegetarian dishes and pickles.

Ginger root is the knobbly root of the ginger plant. It is tough and fibrous and is usually peeled and sliced before use. Dried ginger powder is very different and should not be used as a substitute.

Green mango powder (*amchur*): Amchur is the unripe fruit of the mango tree. The sour green mangos are sliced and dried in the sun, turning a light brown. It has a strong, pungent flavour, and can be bought powdered or in pieces.

Kokum: The kokum tree produces round, purplish plum-like fruit, and it is the skin of the fruit that is used in cooking. When dried, the skins turn a deep black-brown and have a sour, rather salty taste. Like tamarind, kokum is often used as a souring agent.

Mace: The crimson, lacy membrane surrounding the nutmeg seed, is sold dried as

blades. The flavour is similar to that of nutmeg, but is stronger and more pungent. Ground mace deteriorates rapidly.

Mustard is a very important spice in Indian cooking. The brownish-black seeds are used whole and ground in all kinds of dishes and pickles, and the oil extracted from the seeds is used for frying.

Nutmeg is best freshly grated for its sweet, mellow aroma to be used to best effect. Like mace, ground nutmeg deteriorates rapidly.

Paprika is a bright scarlet powder with a sweet, and in the case of Indian paprika, mild taste.

Saffron: The dried stigmas of a variety of crocus is grown in Kashmir, and is the world's most expensive spice. It is available in strands or as powder. It imparts a beautiful deep yellow colour to food, especially rice pilaus and biryanis, lamb dishes and desserts.

Tamarind is a brownish-black, acid-tasting pulpy pod, rather like a pea pod. It is

available compressed into cakes or as juice, and is used mainly as a souring agent and in chutneys and relishes.

Turmeric is a powder obtained from the dried root of a plant belonging to the ginger family. It is used principally as a colouring agent, being much less costly than saffron. Turmeric is sacred to the Hindus.

SPICE MIXTURES

Curry powder, despite its popular association with India, is a Western, and specifically British invention; some brands may be produced in India, but it is almost never used there. The idea of resorting to a commercially mass-produced powder, as opposed to a careful selection of specific spices chosen to complement a particular food, is unthinkable. The better proprietary brands of curry powder are useful and convenient but no commercial blend, however good, can take the place of freshly ground spices or provide the seasoning for a host of dishes which should all taste different. The word curry, which derives from *kari,* a Tamil word for sauce, refers not to the name of a dish but to the technique of stewing with water and spices to form a sauce. Currying is not the ubiquitous cooking method of India; it is just one of the many different Indian cooking techniques. Many areas of India use different characteristic spice mixtures; the mixtures given here represent only a minute selection of the many Indian spice combinations used for currying, but they do exhibit regional variations in terms of heat and emphasis of ingredients.

BOMBAY MIXTURE
4-5 small dried chillies
(to make 1 teaspoon when ground)
1×4-5 cm (1½-2 inch) piece cinnamon stick
4½ tablespoons whole coriander seeds
1 teaspoon whole cumin seeds
½ teaspoon whole fennel seeds
⅔ teaspoon whole fenugreek seeds
½ teaspoon garlic powder or granules
2⅔ teaspoons ground turmeric
2 kokum skins
2 crushed curry leaves

Lightly roast together the first six ingredients; then grind and mix with the garlic and the turmeric. Use according to recipe instructions, adding the kokum skins and the crushed curry leaves directly to the cooking pot, removing the kokum skins before serving.

PANCHPHORAN (BENGALI FIVE SPICES)
This spice mixture originates from Bengal in north-eastern India. Like various other Indian mixes the panchphoran spices are used whole as opposed to ground. It is available as a proprietary brand from Indian grocers, but it may be marketed under 'Five Spices' or 'Five Spice Mixture'. Panchphoran makes an excellent frying spice and can be used to good effect with fish and seafood (crunchy fried prawns, for example), and with meat and poultry.

2 teaspoons whole cumin seeds
2¾ teaspoons whole fennel seeds
1 teaspoon whole fenugreek seeds
1¾ teaspoons whole black mustard seeds
1-2 teaspoons whole nigella (kalonji) seeds

Mix ingredients together.

GARAM MASALA
Garam means hot, and *masala* a blend of spices. This spice mixture is absolutely essential in the cooking of north India. It is usually sprinkled on a dish at the end of cooking, but may also sometimes be added at the beginning or in the course of cooking. Ready-made *garam masala* is available from all Asian food shops, but grinding your own blend of spices for this mixture will make all the difference.

15 g/½ oz black cumin seeds
15 g/½ oz white cumin seeds
75 g/3 oz coriander seeds
40 g/1½ oz brown cardamom seeds
4 bay leaves
50 g/2 oz black peppercorns
15 g/½ oz grated nutmeg
15 g/½ oz blade mace
40 g/1½ oz cinnamon stick

Roast all the spices together as described on page 131 in a heavy frying pan, for about 10 minutes. Grind the spices to a fine powder in a mortar or electric coffee grinder. Store in an airtight container for up to 3 months.

CHICK CHOP SPICE MIXTURE
2 tablespoons coriander seeds
1 teaspoon red chilli powder
6 cloves
2 teaspoons brown cardamom seeds
10 black peppercorns
½ teaspoon black cumin seeds
½ teaspoon white cumin seeds
2×5 cm (2 inch) pieces cinnamon stick
½ teaspoon green cardamom seeds
½ teaspoon ground mace
½ teaspoon grated nutmeg

See page 25 for recipe using this mixture.

TANDOORI MASALA

This is the spice mixture used to rub into whole chickens or pieces of chicken, lamb, etc, cooked in the special clay tandoor oven. Unlike the preceding spice mixtures, the spices in tandoori masala are not roasted first.

1 teaspoon garlic powder
1 teaspoon ground ginger
1 teaspoon ground cloves
1 teaspoon ground mace
½ teaspoon grated nutmeg
2 tablespoons ground coriander
1½ teaspoons ground cumin
1 teaspoon ground fenugreek seeds
1 teaspoon ground cinnamon
1 teaspoon ground black pepper
1 teaspoon ground brown cardamom seeds
2 teaspoons paprika
2 teaspoons red food colouring

Mix together all the ingredients, then push the mixture through a fine sieve. Store in an airtight container for up to 3 months.

TIKKA MIXTURE

¼ teaspoon ground chilli or cayenne
¼-1 teaspoon Garam Masala, to taste
3 garlic cloves, peeled and chopped
1 × 2.5 cm (1 inch) piece chopped fresh ginger root
2 teaspoons chopped fresh coriander leaves (optional)
1 teaspoon ground cumin seeds (optional)
½ teaspoon red food colouring (optional)
1 teaspoon turmeric (or yellow food colouring; both optional)
pepper to taste
1¼ teaspoons salt
2-3 tablespoons lemon juice
6 tablespoons plain unsweetened yogurt

Check individual recipes to see whether lemon juice or salt needs to be used in advance of marinading, whether food needs to be scored and whether colouring should be added at a later stage. Otherwise, combine all ingredients and mix together thoroughly. Brush this marinade all over items to be cooked and leave to marinade for 6 hours or more, depending on size of item. Then follow individual recipe instructions.
Uses: Chicken is certainly the favourite food chosen for tandoori or tikka cooking; although lobster and prawns are also superb. Both chicken and fish *tikkas* are exceptionally good and often eaten as snacks with evening drinks. Serve both tandooris and tikkas on a bed of lettuce, garnished with onion rings, tomato quarters and slices of lemon.

HOT SPICE MIXTURES

SAMBHAR MASALA

This hot spice mixture is used in the cooking of southern India.

50 g/2 oz coriander seeds
20 black peppercorns
½ teaspoon asafoetida powder
8 curry leaves
1½ teaspoons fenugreek seeds
2 teaspoons white cumin seeds
2 teaspoons turmeric powder
2 teaspoons mustard seeds
50 g/½ oz red chillies
2 tablespoons mixed dried black beans, chick peas and lentils

Roast the spices and pulses individually in a heavy frying pan for a few minutes, as described on p. 131. Grind all the ingredients to a fine powder in a mortar or electric coffee grinder. Store in an airtight container for up to 3 months.

VINDALOO MASALA

This fiery spice mixture is used to make the famous hot vindaloo dishes from Goa, in the south-west of India. Vindaloo is traditionally made with pork, which is not eaten very widely in India, except by the Portuguese Christians in Goa, but there are also variations prepared with chicken, beef and lamb.

15 cloves
4 brown cardamom pods, peeled
4 × 5 cm/2 inch pieces cinnamon stick
4 bay leaves
8 dry red chillies
20 black peppercorns
1 tablespoon turmeric powder
1 tablespoon white cumin seeds
1 tablespoon black cumin seeds
4 tablespoons coriander seeds
1½ teaspoons fenugreek seeds
1½ teaspoons mustard seeds

Roast all the spices together in a heavy frying pan, until they give off an aromatic smell – about 10 minutes. Grind to a fine powder in a mortar or electric coffee grinder and store in an airtight container for up to 3 months.

MADRAS MIXTURE

1-3 teaspoons ground chilli
8½ tablespoons ground coriander seeds
3 tablespoons ground cumin seeds
⅛ teaspoon ground ginger
1 teaspoon ground black mustard seeds
1 teaspoon ground fenugreek seeds
1 teaspoon ground black pepper
1⅔ teaspoons ground turmeric
4 whole curry leaves

Mix together all ground dry spices; then proceed according to recipe instructions, adding the curry leaves directly to the cooking pot.

SPECIAL INGREDIENTS

GHEE

Ghee, or clarified butter, is the most popular frying medium in Indian cuisine, giving delicious flavour and crispness to fried food.

450 g/1 lb unsalted butter

1. Cut the butter into small dice. Place in a heavy-based saucepan and set over a very low heat – it should not sizzle – until melted. This will take **5-15** minutes.
2. Raise the heat to moderate, until a thin layer of white foam appears on the surface of the butter. Simmer without stirring for about 10 minutes, until the foam subsides.
3. Stir constantly, watching the pan carefully, until the solids at the base of the pan turn brown. Turn off the heat and skim the scum from the surface.
4. Leave to cool, then strain through a double thickness of muslin into a jar with a screw top. Store in the refrigerator.

BOONDI (batter drops)

Keep these boondi in store to make quick sweetmeats and puddings.

225 g/8 oz gram flour
300 ml/½ pint water
oil for deep frying

1. Gradually mix the water into the flour to make a smooth batter. Whisk well and leave for 10 minutes.
2. Heat the oil in a heavy-bottomed saucepan until a cube of day-old bread turns golden in 1 minute. Using a perforated spoon with round holes, pour the batter into the oil, shaking the spoon so that the batter drops through in pieces.

Use a little of the batter at a time.
3. Use a perforated spoon to turn the boondi and to take them from the oil. Drain the cooked boondi on absorbent kitchen paper and store in an airtight container for future use.

INDIAN YOGURT (*dahi*)

This delicious creamy yogurt, called *dahi,* is an essential ingredient in Indian cuisine, for sauces, marinades, dips, salads and drinks. It makes a delicious dessert, flavoured with rose water or almond essence. The yogurt used in India is made with buffalo's milk. This recipe gives the nearest approximation to the real thing.

600 ml/1 pint creamy milk
2 tablespoons natural yogurt

1. Bring the milk to the boil in a heavy-based saucepan, stirring constantly to prevent a skin from forming on the surface.
2. Remove from the heat and leave to cool for about 10 minutes, until the milk is a temperature of about 130°F/55°C. The milk must not be too hot, otherwise the heat will kill the yogurt culture. Remove any skin from the surface.
3. Beat the yoghurt, then add to the milk, stirring well. Pour from one container to another several times, to produce a frothy surface. Pour into a bowl, cover with a clean tea-towel and leave overnight in a warm place until thickened. Store in the refrigerator.

KHOYA

This dried fresh milk is rather like fudge and is the base for a wide variety of Indian sweetmeats. See pages 114, 121 and 122 for recipes using khoya.

1.2 litres/2 pints milk

1. Bring the milk to the boil in a heavy-based saucepan, stirring to prevent a skin from forming. This stage should take about 15 minutes.
2. Reduce the heat and simmer, stirring to prevent the milk from sticking, until thickened. Stir more vigorously as it gets thicker. This stage will take **45-50** minutes. The khoya is ready when it is reduced to a thick, grainy, very sticky paste that comes away from the sides of the pan.
3. Allow to cool – it will develop a fudge-like texture and consistency and lose its stickiness. Refrigerate in a covered bowl, or wrapped in foil.

SPECIAL GRAVY

This delicious spicy sauce, called *shorwa,* has a number of uses. One is for simmering minced meat balls, or *kofta.*

100 g/4 oz ghee
1 large onion, finely chopped
1 teaspoon turmeric powder
1 teaspoon red chilli powder
1 teaspoon ground coriander
2 cloves garlic, crushed
½ teaspoon grated ginger root
2 tablespoons tomato purée
2 tablespoons natural yogurt
300 ml/½ pint warm water
½ teaspoon salt

1. Heat the ghee in a saucepan, add the onion and fry until golden. Stir in the spices and mix well.
2. Add the tomato purée and yogurt and stir over a gentle heat for about 5 minutes.
3. Add the water and salt, then simmer for 10 minutes.

UNUSUAL INGREDIENTS & FLAVOURINGS

These unusual items are not generally available, but can usually be found in specialist Indian foodstores.

Black salt: A natural spicy salt, brownish black in lump form, and pinkish brown when powdered. It has a tangy taste and smoky aroma.

Chapati flour: A wholesome starch

Chick pea flour: Used in stocks and other foods

Coconut flour: Very fine flour, made from dried, grated coconut. Tastes very strongly of coconut.

Jackfruit: A delicious tasting variety of breadfruit

Jaggery: Unrefined palm sugar, used in pickles

Pigeon peas: Pulses often used in dalls. Native to India, they are also eaten in India and the Caribbean.

Pomegranate seeds: Dried seeds of the pomegranate fruit. Sharp-flavoured and piquant, they are used as a souring agent. Often used in N. India vegetable dishes and considered an essential ingredient in the stuffing for Vegetable Samosas (see page 16).

Rosewater: Aromatic liquid used in sweetmeats and sherbets

Silver foil: Also known as *vark*, this edible foil is used as a decoration on food. It is made from beaten silver dust which is compressed between two sheets of paper. To use, first peel off the top layer of paper. Lift the bottom sheet and invert over the food to be decorated, then gently peel off the paper.

Urad dall flour: Flour made from black beans

Yam: A tuberous root found all over the East. It is cooked the same way as potatoes and has a mild flavour.

Karela: above. Also known as bitter gourd, on account of its taste. In India it is known as 'men's food'. To use, cut in half lengthwise and scoop out the bitter seeds. Sprinkle with salt to sweat out some of the bitterness before cooking.

Kewra essence: An essence extracted from the flowers of the screwpine.

Tindori: above. A small, oval-shaped vegetable with a fresh-tasting, cucumber-like flavour. Use to add freshness to vegetable curries.

Whitegourd: above. A type of sweet-tasting pumpkin, often used in puddings and desserts. See the recipe for Whitegourd Sweetmeat (page 124) from Agra, which is decorated with pieces of silver foil (*vark*) – see above.

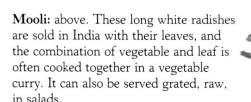

Turia: above. A gourd, also known as angled loofah. To cook, cut in half and scoop out the seeds. Cut into chunks and cook in vegetable curry.

Mooli: above. These long white radishes are sold in India with their leaves, and the combination of vegetable and leaf is often cooked together in a vegetable curry. It can also be served grated, raw, in salads.

Sargowa: above. A long, thin bean-like vegetable, used in curries.

TECHNIQUES

Indian food is unique in its imaginative use of spices, seasoning and flavourings. Many of the cooking techniques are really ways of getting these same spices, seasonings and flavourings to yield as great a variety of tastes and textures as possible. Spices and herbs do not have single, limited tastes. Depending upon the way in which they are used – whole, ground, roasted, fried – they can be coaxed into producing a much larger spectrum of tastes than you might first imagine.

Making thick sauces

Many meat, poultry and fish dishes have thick, dark sauces. There is no flour in these sauces. The 'body' comes, very often, from onions, garlic and ginger. The rich brown colour comes from frying all these ingredients properly. Very often, they make a paste of one or more of these ingredients first. In India, this has been done for centuries on a grinding stone, but in Western kitchens it can be done easily in food processors and blenders, sometimes with the aid of a little water.

Once the paste has been made, it needs to be browned or the sauce will not have the correct flavour and colour. This is best done in a heavy pan, preferably a non-stick pan, in enough oil. Don't worry about burning – it will be all right if you watch it.

Start the frying on a medium-high flame and turn the heat down as the onions lose their liquid and begin to turn brown. They do need to be a rich reddish-brown colour or your sauce – if that is what they are intended for – will be pale and weak.

The same goes for garlic. Garlic tastes quite superb if it is chopped and allowed to fry in oil until it turns a medium-brown colour. You can cook courgettes this way – in oil that has been flavoured with browned garlic. Spinach and cauliflower tastes good this way, too.

Adding yogurt to sauces

Yogurt adds a creamy texture and a delicate tartness to many of our sauces. But yogurt curdles when it is heated. So when you add it to browning sauces, add just a tablespoon at a time. After 1 tablespoon of yogurt has been put in, it is stirred and fried until it is absorbed and 'accepted' by the sauce. Then the next tablespoon is added.

Cooking chicken without its skin

In India, they often remove the skin of the chicken before cooking. The flavour of the spices penetrates the chicken much better this way and the entire dish is less fatty.

Marinating

Cut deep gashes in large pieces of meat or poultry, eg when making tandoori chicken, and leave them in a marinade of yogurt and seasonings. The yogurt tenderizes the meat while the gashes allow the flavour to penetrate deep inside the meat.

TO MAKE KOFTAS

Koftas are similar to minced meat kebabs. They are usually shaped into balls, then simmered in a rich sauce and served as a main dish, with rice. Nargisi Kofta (see recipe on page 83) can best be described as the Indian version of Scotch Eggs – the minced meat mixture is moulded around hard-boiled eggs before being simmered in sauce.

Divide the minced meat mixture into portions. With oiled hands, shape each meat portion into a round, flat shape.

Place the hard-boiled egg in the middle of the meat shape and mould the meat evenly around the shape, making sure there are no thin areas.

TO MAKE SAMOSAS

Samosas are the best-known of the traditional Indian snacks. They are stuffed either with potatoes (*aloo*) or with minced meat (*keema*. See pages 15-16 for recipes). They are fiddly to make, but well worth the effort.

Roll out the pastry into 15 cm (6 inch) circles. Cut each circle in half – each semicircle will make a samosa.

Moisten the edges of the semicircle with water and fold over to form a cone. Press the straight edges firmly together to seal. Place just under a tablespoon of filling each cone.

Moisten the open end of the cone and fold one end over the other, pinching the open end in a straight line. Press tightly to seal.

TO MAKE KEBABS

Kebabs can be made either with small pieces of meat marinated in a fragrant, spicy mixture, or with minced meat flavoured with herbs and spices. For *Seek Kebabs* (see page 92 for recipe) the minced meat is shaped into patties and then moulded around metal skewers – two or three on each skewer. The kebabs are then cooked over a charcoal grill.

Divide the minced meat mixture into equal portions. Flatten slightly. Oil metal skewers and lay across two or three shapes.

Using oiled hands mould the mince patties firmly around the skewer.

PANEER or CHENNA

This curd cheese is widely used in cooking throughout India, in both savoury and sweet dishes. This cheese is known as *paneer* when compressed into a cake and cut into squares.

1.2 litres/2 pints creamy milk
juice of 1 lemon or 2 tablespoons malt
vinegar or 4 tablespoons natural yogurt

1. Bring the milk to the boil in a heavy-based saucepan. Reduce the heat and add the lemon juice, vinegar or yogurt, which will make the milk curdle.

2. Stir gently for up to 1 minute, until the curds separate from the whey. As the curd begins to form, stir very gently so that the curds remain in large lumps and do not break up into small pieces. Turn off the heat immediately.

3. Pour the mixture into a large sieve or colander lined with several thicknesses of muslin. Hold under a gently running cold tap for a few seconds.

4. Bring up the four corners of the muslin and tie together. Twist gently to extract as much moisture as possible, then hang the bag up and leave the cheese to drain for 1½ hours, until crumbly.

5. To make into paneer, place the cheese, still in the muslin bag, on a work surface and shape into a block. Cover with a board and weight down. Leave for 2 hours, then cut into squares.

SUGAR SYRUP

This sugar syrup, called *chaashni*, is used in the preparation of many Indian sweetmeats.

600 ml/1 pint water
450 g/1 lb granulated sugar

1. Mix the water and sugar in a deep, heavy-based saucepan. Bring slowly to the boil, without stirring, until the sugar has dissolved.

2. Lower the heat and simmer, stirring, for about 10 minutes, to 118°C, 245°F, or until a drop of the cooled syrup pressed between your thumb and forefinger forms a soft ball.

DRINKS

Indians don't usually drink while eating, for if curries are too pungent, liquid does little to help. Rice or bread is far better. Also, long drinks after eating rice create a feeling of excessive fullness.

Sherbet

After a meal, when betel cardamom and a little *paan* (a pungent leaf of the cress family) have been chewed to clean the teeth, sweeten breath and aid digestion, guests in India usually sip glasses of sherbet (Arabic *sharbah* from *shariba, to drink;* or Hindi *sharbat*) or cups of spiced tea. Sherbets were introduced by the invading Turks and Persians and are consumed in large quantities as they replace the large loss of body fluids which occurs in a tropical climate.

Originally sherbet was made from fruit juice and snow, but today from any fruit juice, cooled and sweetened and with possibly a little rose water added. Indian sherbet bears no resemblance to the fizzy concoctions sold to children under that name in Britain. The most popular sherbets are made from mango, palm fruit, pineapple lime, etc.

Spiced Teas

Spiced teas usually have a cinnamon, cardamom or mint base and are taken either hot or very cold, usually with sugar but never with milk. They contain herbs and are often flavoured with lime or lemon. In a hot climate they are very refreshing.

Wines, Spirits and Beers

A good, dry sherry goes well before dinner. Try one of the 'finos': a pale Amontillado or salty Manzanilla.

Generally speaking, light beers are the best beverages to drink with or after curries. Sweet, heavy wines do not go well with Indian food – riesling, hock, chablis or graves are best, or cider.

THANDAI (MILK AND SAFFRON SHERBET)

15 g (½ oz) blanched almonds
15 g (½ oz) pistachio nuts
10-12 small green cardamoms, shelled
pinch of saffron fronds
50 g (2 oz) caster sugar (or to taste)
2 pints milk, chilled
¼ teaspoon ground turmeric
¼ teaspoon ground nutmeg or 3 drops nutmeg essence
crushed ice (optional)

Also known as kesher doodh, this is a very popular Indian refreshment and can be made with hot milk, too. In many parts of India, a little alcohol is added, and the sherbet is drunk during festivals such as Holi (festival of spring).

The mixture may be prepared in a large quantity and stored in a sealed jar.
1. Finely grind the almonds, pistachio nuts, cardamoms and saffron fronds.
2. Dissolve the sugar in the milk by stirring thoroughly. Add the turmeric, nutmeg and the ground mixture. Stir well and serve, adding crushed ice, if preferred.

SPICED TEA

1 pint/600 ml water
2 cloves
1 black cardamom pod
4 black peppercorns
2.5 cm/1 inch stick cinnamon
2 teaspoons Indian tea
300 ml/½ pint milk
2 tablespoons sugar

1. Bring the water to the boil in a saucepan with the spices. Add the tea and simmer for 2 minutes.
2. Remove from the heat, add the milk and sugar and serve hot.

ALMOND LASSI

300 ml/½ pint natural yogurt
2-3 tablespoons caster sugar
600 ml/1 pint ice-cold water
8 ice cubes, crushed
4 teaspoons flaked almonds

1. Place all the ingredients except the almonds in a blender and blend until well mixed and frothy.
2. Pour into tumblers and sprinkle with the almonds. Serve immediately.

SPICED WATER

225 g/8 oz seedless tamarind pulp (see p. 131)
900 ml/1½ pints warm water
3 tablespoons salt
2 teaspoons sugar
2 large dry red chillis
1 teaspoon grated root ginger
1 tablespoon chopped mint
1 tablespoon lemon juice

Spice mixture
a pinch of asafoetida powder
2 teaspoons white cumin seeds
2 teaspoons coriander seeds
2 teaspoons aniseeds
15 black peppercorns

1. Soak the tamarind in one-third of the water for 30 minutes. Rub the pulp through a fine nylon sieve into a jug. Add the remaining water.
2. Roast all the spices in a dry frying pan (see page 131), then grind with all the remaining ingredients except for the lemon juice to make a smooth paste.
3. Gradually stir the spice paste into the tamarind mixture, shaking the jug as you do so. Add the lemon juice, stir well again and chill in the refrigerator, before serving topped up with ice cubes.

MENU PLANNER

DINNER PARTIES

Vegetarian minestrone (page 8)

Fish in coconut milk (page 64)

Spinach in skinless black beans (page 44)

Chicken biriyani (page 68)

Puri stuffed with dhal (page 96)

Batter coils in syrup (page 118)

Ginger soup (page 15)

Rogan josht (page 59)

Prawn curry (page 59)

Marrow kofta curry (page 51)

Naan (page 99)

Tomato chutney (page 107)

Yogurt sherbet (page 122)

VEGETARIAN SUPPERS

Stuffed aubergines (page 36)

Cauliflower curry (page 43)

Vegetable biriyani (page 26)

Lentils (page 26)

Chapatis (page 96)

Carrot preserve (page 111)

Coconut pudding (page 118)

Potatoes in green coriander (page 19)

Aubergine raita (page 107)

Plain rice pullao (page 22

Marrow kofta curry (page 51)

Paratha stuffed with radish (page 100)

Pigeon pea purée (page 22)

Banana and satsuma pudding (page 121)

BARBECUE

Minced meat samosas (page 15)

Pork tikka (page 91)

Grilled drumsticks (page 68)

Gooseberry chutney (page 107)

Cream cheese kofta (page 47)

Poppadums (page 100)

LIGHT LUNCHES

Indian scrambled eggs (page 12)

Chapatis (page 96)

Jackfruit curry (page 32)

Yam foogath for the brave (page 16)

Naan (page 99)

Stuffed crabs (page 59)

Cocktail curry (page 48)

Nuggets of lamb (page 80)

Puri stuffed with dhal (page 96)

Haddock croquettes (page 63)

Fried cabbage (page 35)

BUFFET SUPPER

Potato chaat (page 11)

Vegetable samosas (page 16)

Pea and cream cheese pullao (page 29)

Lamb kebabs (page 92)

Bengali fish curry (page 63)

Chicken korma (page 72)

Lemon pickle (page 111)

Mango chutney (page 104)

Parathas (page 99)

Chapatis (page 96)

Crumbly deep-fried bread (page 96)

Blackberry sherbet (page 124)

Gram flour diamonds (page 114)

INDEX

ACKNOWLEDGEMENTS

Photography
IAN O'LEARY

Photographic styling
CAROLYN RUSSELL

Preparation of food for photography
ANNE HILDYARD

Illustrations
ALISON WISENFELD

Step-by-step illustrations
PATRICIA CAPON

Map illustration
EUGENE FLEURY

Cover photography
VERNON MORGAN

Preparation of food for cover photography
ALLYSON BIRCH